PERSEVERANCE

—————— *of* ——————

Yesterday's Women

DRAGANA DJURDJEV

PAGE PUBLISHING, INC.
New York, NY

First originally published by Page Publishing, Inc. 2017

ISBN 978-1-64138-367-7 (Paperback)
ISBN 978-1-64138-368-4 (Digital)

Printed in the United States of America

DEDICATION

I dedicate this book to everyone who touched my life while I was in pain and feeling destroyed. I thank God, who is always present in my life, who heard my prayers and sent me friends and strangers to help me with my needs. I would like to thank my daughters for becoming wonderful women and for blessing me with six grandsons whose sweet faces and unconditional affection warm my heart every day.

I send love to the friends and strangers whose kindness and counsel rescued me when I was in despair and shared my joy when I freed my soul. Most of all, I thank them for their kindness that breathed life into me. Thank you, dear Casandra, Connie, Barbara, and Mary Ann, for your support and persistence. Without you, this book would never have been written.

I dedicate this story to all the young women who are open-minded and brave enough to want to learn from yesterday's women who lived challenging lives, and to all of yesterday's women who are brave and willing to look back and share the lessons they learned while on their journey. At times, you may doubt my story, but God is my witness that I foolishly endured it instead of changing it. I had more faith in my ex-husband's power than in mine and God's. Life has a pattern, and the pattern comes from yesterday's woman in each of our lives. There wouldn't be a book to write or a book to read if there wasn't a brave mother, grandmother, great-grandmother . . .

Knowledge and courage help us determine the best possible path to take while on our life's journey. Without knowledge and courage, we enable others to hijack our life and force us to join them on their journey in emotional bondage.

If you see yourself in my story, I hope you see my power as well and say to yourself out loud, "I can do it," then plan to do whatever *it* is you want to do. Life is short; don't allow anyone to live it for you. With this story, I send you courage.

—Dragana DJurdjev

Life is not always lived, as planned

My thoughts constantly bubbling at speed for years – invited me to write a personal story I have long wanted to write, but for which I have always lacked the necessary strength and a period of time when life was not in a state of turbulence... and in that ellipsis, I engaged in a lengthy debate with myself as to whether to reveal, with complete honesty, the events I wish to record, and I have decided that this manuscript would be as worthless as a leaf floating in the fall winds if I resorted of fiction, even fiction by omission. So I told the entire truth on these pages, even if this causes me the greatest pain – and it will, it will.

The prose chipped and crackling is simply evidence of a life once lived, the proof that I once passed this way and sought to have love and understanding, passion and forgiveness, if not finally for my soul which is always yearning and wanting.

Upon rereading this memoir, I see that I have revealed more than I intended, both to the reader and myself; I see perhaps while strangers may gain enlightenment, it may cause discomfort to the children and friends; To all I say, no matter what, we must keep in mind a life is lived as it unfolds not as we plan it.

CONTENTS

INTRODUCTION

I write my story as my heart recalls the events, regardless if they were painful, joyful, challenging, or gratifying. While writing, I've learned many things about myself as I was in the past and the type of person I have become as a result of all my experiences and the people I met along the way. I hope the readers will enjoy sharing my journey as I gained wisdom and became *yesterday's woman.*

Having God as my constant companion, I realized he answered my prayers for strength to free myself by sending friends and strangers whose words and kindness lifted me up and carried me from despair to spiritual freedom and joy.

My christened name is Dragana Djurdjev. A kind teacher, Ms. Freeman, thought that was an ideal name for teasing, so she renamed me Ann. Like many foreigners, when I became a citizen, I accepted that name as my legal name.

I chose to write this book in hope that those in the teaching profession will see how valuable and critical they are to any child, especially to the children who are foreign in the United States or in their own homes. Bless you all who are teachers. Please seek to be like yesterday's women and teach from your heart with kindness—you might save a lost soul like Ms. Freeman and Mrs. Whitehorn saved me.

To look back through my past is sometimes scary and shattering, yet still I choose to tough it out and tell my story in hope that those who see a similar pattern in their relationships say out loud to themselves, "I am not going to wait twenty-seven years like Ann to get my life back!"

I send you courage.

I will start my story by sadly admitting that all my life's changes for the good and the bad were marked by my husband's dalliances and betrayals, which make it impossible for me not to talk about him as much as I will talk about myself. This style of telling a story will make sense to all women who are involved with difficult and troubled men. If you are not involved in a relationship, please make this a cautionary tale. If you are married and your story is similar to mine, know that you do not need to and you should not stay in an abusive and controlling, lonely environment. In the sixties, people turned their heads when they witnessed spousal abuse. Today, there are many places to seek help. If you feel you need it, please seek it. We have only one life to live; don't give it away like I did.

One day, I woke up and realized everything that was critical to me as a human being was in ruins. All I could see in my reality was a shattered life. It was like seeing myself in a shattered mirror. I sacrificed for others everything important for a person's survival, and in return, all that was left was a shattered, smoldering life. Terrified, alone, I lit a candle, said a prayer, and said to myself out loud, "It is okay. I am free. I am not alone, God is with me." From that moment on, God was, and still is, my constant companion.

I was not inclined to discuss all the pain with friends or my mother; instead, I sought knowledge. It seemed like I read a million books while getting ready to free myself, and in so doing, I decided the best course of action would be to return to college and get a degree in psychology. That seemed like my only hope and resource to figure out how to rebuild myself and sort out pain from goodness in me. I knew that knowledge would enable me to choose the best paths while on my journey for the remaining years of my life. Along the way, in books, I learned concepts of the human mind, but yesterday's women helped me unlock the secrets of the human soul.

Studying human development psychology set me free and made me realize that although I could not right any wrongs, I could unchain myself from all the wrongs by gaining understanding of myself through my mother's and my grandmother's experiences. They were my yesterday's women. They had the answers.

I wrote this book as advice to all those who are cognizant that they are on someone else's journey and feel lost and in pain. I encourage you to dedicate some time to yourself to gather your courage and enter the fear den called the past then methodically sort out all the painful and unkind memories and place them in a closet in your mind and lock the door. I warn you, you will have to run through that den of fear many times until you pull out good memories and your successes. It will be scary! It will be like pulling your favorite pet out of a fire, scary and painful, but you *can* do it.

I will begin to tell you my story now, and in the end, I hope you will see that the journeys of yesterday's women like me, your mother, or your grandmother set the pointers to safe paths we must take as we move forward on our personal journeys. We are doomed to fail if we do not listen to the wisdom they gained from their experiences. Their wisdom is food for our souls as we grow our power.

Peers are valuable. If they are your age, generally speaking, they, too, are searching for the right paths to a peaceful journey. However, they only know the road they have traveled or that they are currently on. Yesterday's Women possess a map marked by experience that can help you differentiate the safe versus the treacherous road. They know which roads lead to sunshine or darkness. Take time to seek their counsel. Listen to their stories, and you will be enlightened.

Sadly, I didn't listen.

CHAPTER ONE

CHILDHOOD IN YUGOSLAVIA

Dear reader, as you read this story, do not be sad for me. I, like a pilot, had to take lessons to fly. Like life, lessons are not free, and sometimes the ride is bumpy. Read on. In the second part of my story, I became an expert, and you will enjoy flying with me. You may even learn from me how to fly.

I have been Ann since I came to the United States in 1957. I was born in 1947, just as World War II was ending.

Where does one's story begin?

I've asked that question to myself many times. As I searched for the answer, I realized the answer for me was not my birth date or the many stories told to me by my family members.

The first glimpse of my existence unfolds in my memory like a story told in a movie. Oddly, my first awareness of myself is related to my mother. I see myself for the first time in a short little white dress with a bow in my hair, standing on the sidewalk, eagerly waiting for the trolley that stops in front of my grandmother's home. I wait with great excitement for the trolley to pull in and come to a stop. With a child's excitement, I wait for a woman I think is beautiful, always smiling, always giving me hugs, bringing a tiny, little surprise, a piece of fruit or a candy. I wait for the trolley exit door to open and for her to step down from the last step. Although this woman is my mother, that memory does not identify her as my mother, only as a beautiful woman, with dark curly hair and big smile, so happy to see me standing at the platform as she steps down from the trolley step. She hugs me, lifts me up, puts me down, takes my little hand in hers, and walks us home. My records suggest I am four years old.

I have only a few memories of my childhood, yet they are of her, my mother. I recall my delight in hearing her laughter, seeing her beauty, her vibrancy. I see her opening all the windows and the front door, singing as she cleans the small three-room house where we live with my grandparents. She is singing most beautifully. I see her, I hear her call me by my pet name, Gaco, but I can't hear myself calling her Mommy, or Mom, or recall ever doing so. I don't know why that is.

I would eventually get the answer from my stepfather a year after my mother's death.

After the age of four, I could not recall seeing this beautiful, loving woman, my mother. Her name was Vera Glisic. I was too young to wonder where she went, when she left, why she left, or when she would be back. I wouldn't get those answers until I was ten years old.

Why She Left: This Was When I Began to Pay for the Sins of the Father

For the reader to understand the cost of the sins of my father, I will have to begin with my mother's story.

I was born in 1947 in a country formerly known as Yugoslavia. Yugoslavia was a forced merging of several small countries by communist dictator Tito. Serbia was one of those conquered small countries. The Serbian people, as a practical matter, were guided by Eastern Orthodox religious beliefs. In 1947, Eastern Orthodox was a binding religion strictly based on the Old Testament Bible teachings. The powerful information in these teachings grossly changed the course of my grandparents', my parents', and my life.

As I tell my story, it is important to keep in mind one point, and that is that the Serbian people were strictly guided by Eastern Orthodox religious beliefs. My grandparents were obedient, religious people, so when my mother married my sin-driven father, the unraveling of all our lives began. It is important to say that I continued this unraveling by marrying a replica of my sin-driven father. No, I did not listen to the warnings of *yesterday's woman*, my mother.

My mother, Vera, was seventeen when she married my father, a horribly irresponsible man. I will let you judge for yourself as I lay out his evil deeds that weaved through and ruined many lives, especially my mother's. She was young. I can tell you, in those days, women married without knowing anything about life. They lived within tightly bound house rules. Naïveté was their guiding principle. Naïveté gives permission for evil people to use and destroy the innocent. I know this to be true as it relates to my mother and myself, because I followed in her footsteps.

My father's name was Peter. In years, he was only about four years older than Vera; in experience, he was light-years away. He was a well-known horse jockey. His celebrity was an invitation to every party. He was good-looking and charming, as a sociopath can be—no cares, no worries, just did what he fancied. I use this description of him because he continued this behavior with all four of his subsequent wives. We lived in a very small town a few miles outside of Belgrade, capital of Serbia. Everyone knew everyone intimately. So in this very small town, the talk about my father's indiscretions reached my grandfather with the speed of lightning. The humiliation set in just as quickly. When I was about two years old, evidence of my father's indiscretion came to fruition: a bar singer was impregnated by him. This news began my grandparents', my mother's, that of the illegitimate child who was about to be born out of wedlock, and my ascension into hell. From that day forward, none of us knew peace. My mother was affected until her dying day. I am sixty-nine years old as I write this story, and I find I am still affected. The illegitimate child, as he was known in our town, lived an abusive childhood. He was abused and neglected by his mother and her revolving-door boyfriends during all his childhood days. No help or support from Peter.

This disgrace happened just after the Second World War ended. My grandparents lost their businesses during the war, and being poor was the prevailing existence for most people unless they belonged to Tito's Communist Party, so for the Serbian people, their religion and their family pride were all they had to hold on to. The disgrace my father brought on my mother was unbearable for the family and deadly for my young mother. I won't say much more about this situation except that at this point, my mother entered hell, and no matter how hard she worked, how much she accomplished, how close she came to the doorway, she never escaped from that hell. She stayed in hell until she passed away at the age of sixty-six.

For my young mother, there was no viable option to escape what was about to take over her life. Staying in the marriage was not an option, and getting a divorce would bring down the whole family. My grandfather could not take the shame and disgrace, and he berated and shamed my mother. Divorce is not accepted in the Serbian Eastern Orthodox religion now. My grandfather was relentless in his abuse of her. In retrospect, what could she have done about the reckless actions of this husband, an unruly, undisciplined man? There are no consequences for someone like Peter. God knows to this day, there are no real consequences for cheating men or the women they cheat with; there are only consequences for wives and the children.

At least nowadays a woman has viable opportunities to rid themselves of the cheaters without the abuse and stigma from the church and the family.

Once divorced, Vera took a job and tried to reclaim her life. She was forced to move in with my grandparents, with me tagging along. My grandparents lived next door to my sweet aunt and kind uncle. My aunt and uncle had three children, Dusan, Maria, and Bisa, in that order. I was the same age as Maria. Until I was ten years old, it never dawned on me that these three children were my cousins rather than my brother and sisters. To this day, I refer to them as siblings. I don't remember a time when I was ever treated differently by my aunt and uncle or the cousins. We ate together, we went to school together, we played together, and we all got spanked by the uncle, no exceptions.

We all lived by the trolley stop. I don't remember my mother before or after the memory I described in the beginning of this chapter.

From my conversations in later years with my mother, my aunt, and my cousins, it was apparent that Grandfather's shame of my mother's situation made it unbearable for her to retrieve her life. She was divorced and with a child, although not her fault. She might as well have worn a scarlet letter on her chest.

Well, here we are. I need to digress a little back to that Eastern Orthodox, Old Testament religious harness and Grandfather's pride. She was divorced and, worse, with a child. In the wisdom of the respected religious people—I use these words loosely—no respectable man who was never married would ever marry a divorced woman with a child because, by their wisdom, she was simply on the level of a whore. So sad, this belief. Thank God we have at least moved away from labeling the women this way.

It was shortly after we moved in with my grandparents that my mother met Roy. She thought he would be her ticket to freedom, but instead, he was the limousine that took her to the point of no return, to hell. Roy was ultimately to become my stepfather. Roy was a sad, pitiful, wife-beater. He was from one of those God-fearing Serbian Eastern Orthodox families, once again, I say sardonically, who believed their pure son could not marry a divorced woman, especially one with a child. Oh, the religious hypocrites of the era!

I was told by Roy, after the death of my mother, who served him literally in every way—he never cooked a meal, never changed a diaper, etc., for about forty-seven years—that if he knew my mother was divorced or had a child, he would never have married her. This man went to church every Sunday and never developed an ounce of humanity or integrity or appreciation of how much she carried him. How could he say that? You may be wondering. I wondered about that myself.

Why I Don't Remember Calling Vera Mommy or Mom

So now you, the reader, and I not only wonder why I couldn't remember ever calling Vera Mommy or Mom. We now also wonder how Roy could date Vera, come to my grandmother's house to pick her up, yet years later, after her death, state that if he knew my mother was divorced or had a child, he would never have married her. Mercy, when he first made that statement, I thought he must have had his head up his ass, which appeared to be true all the days of his life. I am confident, as my story unfolds, you will come to the same conclusion on your own.

At this juncture, we need to recall my statement of the memory when I would meet Vera at the trolley, overjoyed at her smiling face, and then suddenly, those meetings stopped. I wondered for many years about this in my adult life. I later found out from my aunt that when Vera started to date Roy, I was not to call her mommy. When he would come to our house (that is, my grandparents' house), I was whisked off to my aunt's house. He only knew me as one of the four children at my aunt's house. They all knew, if he found out my mother was divorced, with a child, he would stop seeing her, and to her, he was her ticket to a better life. Lord only knows how wrong she was.

I will digress again to tell you a little more about Yugoslavia and Tito, the dictator. Under Tito's rule, like in any other Communist country, in Yugoslavia, only the members of his Communist Party had wealth, food, and shelter; the rest of the population lost everything when he came into power. Jobs were scarce. When jobs are scarce, so are food and shelter. My mother and I slept in the same bedroom with Grandfather and Grandmother. I would not go too deeply into the politics at this point, only to say that everyone who could defect from Yugoslavia did. And leaving became my mother's goal, with urgency. Roy was part of a bicycling team representing Yugoslavia in the European championships. This position afforded him a visa to travel outside of Yugoslavia. My mother was an equipment buyer for the Yugoslavian government, which enabled her to also get a visa to travel outside of Yugoslavia. In short, they needed each other to leave the country, and leave the country they did. They defected to Austria. I was left behind with my grandparents, aunt and uncle, and the cousins. I was dumb and happy at this point, because I wouldn't have wanted to leave my brother and sisters. A child's naïveté.

Shortly after they defecting to Austria, my mother married Roy, and shortly after that, Vera gave birth to her son, Zoran. I believe this was when she started jumping back and forth from the frying pan into the fire.

In those days, post-World War II, about 1955, jobs were hard to find, even in Austria. And so they decided to leave Austria. Foreigners had to have someone vouch for them to come to America. Roy had an uncle in America who filed the papers for my mother and Roy to come to the States. Shortly after their arrival to the States, Vera delivered a premature baby girl, Zorica.

After my half-sister, Zorica, was born, Vera's life become unbearable. She was alone in the States. Roy was not a hard-working, overtime-doing, two-jobs kind of guy. They now had an unruly thirteen-month-old boy and a premature five-week-old little girl. No one to help with the children, money was tight, language barrier devaluing their skills. Unbearable stress mounted for both Vera and Roy, and sadly, Roy expressed his rage by beating his wife.

I knew nothing about all this because I was dumb and happy in Yugoslavia. I was led to believe, either by their acceptance and inclusion or my own desire, that Dusan, Maria, and Bisa were my siblings, but instead, they were my cousins. I fit right in. When there was fun to be had, I was included equally. When there was discipline to be had, I was treated equally by my uncle, who was the disciplinarian. We lived in a small town, Čukarica. Everyone knew everyone. It was not unusual for me to be loved and disciplined by a teacher or a neighbor. Teacher Zlata talked to Grandmother about my fidgety behavior or disciplined me by ruler on the hand. Our next-door neighbors Tika and Ceda, two men who had lived right next door and grew up with my mother, acted like my uncles. And so on. Grandmother was my whole world—her soft voice, her soft hugs, her protectiveness. My childhood was full of mischief with my cousins and schoolmates. I was embraced with love and kindness. In retrospect, I realized I was everyone's charge, a little, miniature orphan girl everyone liked to park on their lap.

March 1957: My World Was Shattered

One day in March 1957, my grandmother was crying and asked me to sit with her for a talk. I was not quite ten years old then. The contents of that one conversation shattered my world, propelled me from a sheltered world full of love into a world of never-ending toil and pain. It was the beginning of the end of my childhood.

Dragana at the age she was meeting her mother at the trolley.

Dragana's mother Vera just before she left Serbia.

CHAPTER TWO

ARRIVAL IN AMERICA

It was 1957. I was ten years old, still in Serbia. As my mother's world in Chicago, Illinois, became unbearable, what with two infants, language barrier, and no one to help her, she ordered my grandmother to start my paperwork and physical to come to America to help her. I didn't know any of this. I was happy and safe with my aunt and uncle, siblings, grandfather, and grandmother. Grandmother was soft-spoken, huggy, and kind. She was everything to me. So when she sat me down in March of 1957, crying, I was alarmed.

My grandmother was sitting with her hands on her lap and her head down so that I could not see her crying. I asked her if she was crying, and she said no, but I could see she was and I was alarmed. She said, "I have some good news for you. Your mother wants you to come to live with her in America."

I was propelled out of my seat. I told her my brother should go first—he was older. I could not connect then that my cousin was not my sibling; therefore, I could not connect that we did not have the same mother. So now I found out my cousins were not my siblings at the same time I found out there was a mother that was just mine in some place called America. I was screaming with panic, pleading for her not to let me go, to not make me leave, for her to go with me. She was hugging me and reaffirming that only I must go.

The contents of that one conversation shattered my world, propelled me from a sheltered world full of love into a world of never-ending toil and pain. It was the ending of my childhood and the beginning of being a ten-year-old caretaker of two infants and a distraught mother who was beaten and abused by a short-tempered, mean-spirited man, Roy.

As I was preparing, to make me feel better, my grandmother told me my father was also in America. Really, who cared? He never wrote me or sent me anything. She told me he would come see me to make sure I was okay. I didn't know him, and I didn't care to meet him now.

She told me I would have fun, that I had a baby brother and sister. But I was becoming inconsolable.

Each day, while Grandmother was preparing for my departure, I became more desperate. I was begging her not to make me go. With each preparation step, like a physical exam, shots, passport pictures, I felt fear trickle through me. I was distraught.

May 1957 came, and it was then I must leave everyone. I must get on this thing called an airplane. I must go to some place called America, to live with a mother I could not recall anything about.

I was dressed in a pair of pants sized down from my brother's outgrown pants. I was wearing a little sweater, and I was at the airport, begging Grandmother not to make me go. These were times when unaccompanied children traveled alone in the care of the stewardesses. I was checked in like baggage with a sign pinned on my chest to ensure I didn't get lost. I was in a panic.

Fifty-nine years later, as I am writing, tears fill my eyes. I can still feel the panic and the loss I felt of leaving my beloved grandmother.

I was traveling from Belgrade, Serbia, to Paris, France, where I would then board a connecting flight that would take me to my destination, Chicago, Illinois, where my mother and stepfather had settled. In Paris, I was placed in a little room for several hours, eternity to a child, until a stewardess came to take me to my Chicago flight. I was in shock, and I was crying. I couldn't stop crying. I was given medicine to calm me down. It must have been a sleep aid, because the next thing I knew, I heard the stewardess waking me up, telling me we were arriving at the Chicago Midway International Airport.

I was already in a bad state, and when the stewardess walked me off the airplane and into the airport, I lost my mind. I was screaming with panic. When I left Serbia, I had just started fourth grade. We were learning about different countries and history. When we learned about people in China, we learned that one of their unique characteristics was that their eyes were narrow. When we learned about people in Africa, we learned their unique characteristic was that their skin was black. So you can imagine my added panic when I reached the arrival gate and saw gates full of black people. I immediately started pulling the stewardess back into the airplane, screaming at her that she took me to the wrong country—I was not supposed to be in Africa. The Midway Airport area was where African Americans settled, as did other nationalities. But I did not know that. Finally, my mother recognized me and came to pick me up. I saw her—she was still beautiful—and she cried when she saw me. I wanted to love her, but my panic was too overwhelming.

Briefly I calmed down as we walked to claim my baggage— not much was in the suitcase. We were poor. I only had old paja-mas and a dress I inherited from my sister Maria, not because she had many more than I did, but because she had outgrown it. I remember these two items only because they made me feel like some children feel about their favorite original teddy bear. The dress was Maria's, and she was dear to me. She still is.

What was your childhood like?

Dragana's family on the day of her departure for the United States from Belgrade, Serbia in 1957.

CHAPTER THREE

CHILDHOOD IN AMERICA
Pre-High School, 1958–1961

I looked at her face closely for the first time when we arrived at the luggage claim area, and I thought to myself, *She is so beautiful and so sad.* She remained beautiful and sad for the rest of her life. She was never the smiling Vera I remembered as she was when she was stepping off the trolley exit steps in Serbia.

I loved her dearly, but her unhappiness and mine always got in the way of us showing how much we loved each other. As I write this sentence, I am crying from the sadness for her.

It is safe to say that the day I arrived in my mother and Roy's apartment was the last day of my childhood. Gone were the carefree days when I played with my brother and sisters in Serbia, when we would take the train to the farms during the summers to pick fruit or corn for days, and frolic with school friends; when I would swim in the Sava River, tease my friends, make dolls out of matchsticks and thread with my sisters, and occasionally claim our grandfather from the local tavern on payday. Gone was the comfort of knowing everyone loved me and looked after me because I was a petite lighthearted, lovable child- when everyone was my parent.

My childhood was replaced by adulthood the very next day I arrived in Chicago. My mother was stretched to the max emotionally and physically. I had no way of knowing or gauging her situation and emotions; after all, I was accustomed to a quiet aunt and uncle. I had never heard them argue. I had never heard my aunt or grandmother raise their voices.

As my parents told their stories, it was apparent the immigrants I met came to the United States with great hope that they would make a better life for themselves. But the language was a relentless barrier for all of them. No matter how skilled or educated they all were, the lack of English prohibited them from working in their fields of expertise, so they ended up working any job, any hour they could. This was true in Vera and Roy's case. In Yugoslavia, Roy was an electrician, but now he worked in a factory during the day, and because of the two babies, Vera went to clean offices and bathrooms during the night. As their life progressed, Roy never absorbed the hardships. Vera always had to. She used to tell me on several occasions how afraid she was to walk the dangerous streets at midnight when she left her work. Her doctor told her the job she was doing and her stressful life and fear-filled walks from work at midnight through dangerous neighborhoods contributed to her hemorrhaging and having to deliver Zorica prematurely, almost losing her life and the baby in the process. Roy was a limited man in emotion and smarts. Vera was a bright, hardworking woman, and most people who met her liked her. In the end, the reader will most likely draw that conclusion as my story unfolds.

Vera and Roy lived in a small one-bedroom basement apartment on Pulaski Street. Not the best part in the city. In fact, at this time, it was a scary part of Chicago. My half-brother Zoran's crib was in the bedroom with his parents. Good thing that I was a tiny little thing (I still am only five feet tall); my size enabled me to sleep in a small youth bed that was bigger than a crib and smaller than a twin bed. My bed was placed in a walk-in, pantry-size room. Because there was not enough room for my half-sister Zorica's bassinette to be placed in the small area where my bed was located, it was placed outside my doorway. She was a tiny, little premature baby, almost six months old, when I arrived.

On top of all my challenges, I was used to sleeping in crowded rooms with my cousins and, often, in my grandparents' room. Now I must sleep alone in a foreign, dark room, with no windows. Not long after the lights went out and everyone was in bed, I worked myself into an inconsolable panic. Sort of like buyer's remorse; only I couldn't return the change of life. Vera was already tired from working nights, picking me up at the airport, and being sleep-deprived from the babies, and now I was hysterical. It wasn't long before she lost her patience and went from reassuring and pleading to hitting me to calm me down. I can honestly say I still remember that culmination of events and emotion, which only served to cause me to panic more. I did not have self-soothing skills. It went like this for some time. When I did sleep, it was from exhaustion.

I pleaded with her to return me to my grandmother.

In retrospect, I knew she longed for my grandmother to come to help us both. I couldn't eat. Everything I ate, I couldn't digest. When I arrived, I was tiny, and now I was skeletal. From my nerves, I was beginning to develop welts. I visited a Serbian-speaking doctor, and he helped me stop with the vomiting and the general recovery of my health. Shortly after my doctor's visit, Vera told me I was supposed to be her support, and instead, I was an added burden. As months went by, I stopped begging her to send me back to my grandmother, Nana. I redirected myself from hopelessness to hope that my Nana would soon join Vera and me in America.

Hope is a peacemaker.

When I left Serbia, I was starting fourth grade. I was good in many subjects, and I was excellent in math. When I arrived, I expected to finish fourth grade, but instead, I did not go to school at all the first year I arrived in the States. Because of Vera's financial circumstances and the two babies, I had to stay home that year to help take care of the children while Vera worked nights and slept during the day.

By not going to school, I had no peer contact, which heightened my loneliness and isolation. So I turned to Zorica. I took care of her every need, day and night. She was a good baby. I immersed myself in her care. I didn't take to Zoran's care as much as he was older (thirteen months) and harder to care for. My ability to take care of the children developed. Before I knew it, I was taking care of the children and cooking meals when Vera needed time to rest.

A year after my arrival, Roy's uncle helped him get a job as an electrician, and Vera found a job in a factory. Both jobs increased their salaries, which enabled them to move us to a bigger apartment, in a better neighborhood. We moved into a two-bedroom apartment, and I shared the bedroom with the babies.

Just after this move, the new school year started, and I was enrolled in fourth grade again. I should have gone into fifth grade then; however, because I did not finish fourth grade when I arrived and because of the language barrier, it was decided I should start with fourth grade. Like with many foreigners, my name was challenging to pronounce or read. And children can be brutal. My name was Dragana, and to American children, this was a good teasing name, a great name for a dragon, they thought. I didn't mind the teasing; I was very lonely for my brother and sisters and my childhood friends, so I found teasing endearing. I was just elated to be in school, to communicate with children my age. Since I started fourth grade, I had always loved school principally for the social aspect. The minute I met my teacher, Ms. Freedman, her kind voice and soft face warmed my little heart. Ms. Freedman, may God bless her, wherever she is in heaven, turned out to have the most patient and considerate soul. The name-calling and teasing bothered her, so she renamed me Ann. This was when I started to believe that God himself was helping me. With the help of Ms. Freedman, I thrived scholastically and emotionally. She helped me advance my English and motivated other children to work with me. I was advanced in math, and she rewarded me by recognizing me in front of my peers. In the school arena, I was thriving. I was elated to leave the house every day and go to school. In contrast, however, my homelife was eerie and scary. I was apprehensive to go home after school. Every day was different: stress, wife-beatings, blaming, yelling, babies crying.

With the new jobs, both Roy and Vera worked day shifts. The kids went to day care, money was tight, and the family skeletons had begun to come out of the closet. I was beginning to see hope for Vera and myself because it looked like we were going to bring my grandmother to live with us, to help with the children. Meanwhile, Roy's mother had other plans. Remember the story I told about snooty religious hypocrisy? That no unmarried man would marry a divorced woman? With the audacity of a religious hypocrite, Roy's mother decided my mother was not worthy of her son because she was a divorcee, and she refused to recognize their marriage and demanded Roy's uncle find Roy a single Serbian woman. Think about that insanity in his family. Meanwhile, Roy and Vera were married in Austria and had two children. This horrible idea brought about incredible fighting between Roy and Vera. At times, he beat her until she could not stand up. I would be hiding the small children in the bedroom while trying to stop him. He beat my mother intermittently until I started high school, at which point I informed him I had several male friends who were on the football team and would come to protect me and Vera. He put the beatings on hold until I left the house.

It was at this juncture that I knew one thing: no man would ever hit me and live to tell about it!

A Life-Altering Event for Vera and Me

One day, Roy and Vera had a terrible fight, during which he beat her bloody, placed her in the tub, and ran cold water over her to revive her. I thought he was drowning her, and in my panic, I told him I would call the police if he did not stop. I must say to all who read this story, there is no greater terror than to watch your mother helplessly as she is attacked, beaten. It is a special terror if you are a twelve-year-old child with no family to turn to for help. I mention this particularly brutal beating because it became a catalyst that devastated and subsequently changed Vera for the rest of her life.

If you are an educator, I urge you to discuss abuse in the household to your students to create opportunities for children to learn that it is not acceptable and to prevent children from accepting household abuse as the norm.

If you are a woman who is beaten, grab a friend and tell your story. Get help and get out of the relationship. Know that there is always someone like me who will give you understanding and help.

After this terrible event, Vera cleaned up. Having no one to turn to, she wrote a letter to her mother, whom she adored. While she was writing, she was crying. A short time after my mother sent the letter, my aunt notified my mother that Grandmother died of a heart attack. My aunt reported that my grandmother read the letter, which upset her terribly, and took a walk, and when she returned, she collapsed and died from a heart attack. When my mother heard the news, she was inconsolable. She was grief-stricken. She couldn't calm down, she couldn't eat, and she couldn't go to work. She was inconsolable that she lost her mother, more so sick at the thought that she might have contributed to her death. It was then that I realized my mother missed my grandmother as much as I did, that she longed for her to come to live with us, and that she was as much Vera's lifeline as she was mine.

From this time forward, I worked diligently to support Vera in any way I could, including constantly living on edge to keep peace for crazy Roy. He would get upset if the children cried, if the food was not warm enough, if the food was too hot—petty things, just to take his temper out on her and, eventually, on all the children, particularly Zoran.

Peter, the False Savior

To cause more confusion and add a jealously component to this marriage, entered Peter, my long-lost father. Hearing of my grandmother's death and that I was in the States, my father contacted me. Peter loved my grandmother like his mother, and she felt the same about him. She loved the horse races. When he was a horse jockey, they were thick as thieves. Many times, our food money came from my grandmother's horse race winnings. As a twelve-year-old thrown into incredible turmoil, I thought, surely, he would be our savior, especially mine. To understand how terribly wrong I was, I am compelled to write a brief story about Peter that will explain why he was more the devil than the savior.

I am sure Peter's picture is next to the saying in the Bible, "The children pay for the sins of the father," because he created many sins for the children he sired, certainly not fathered. The story told by my fraternal grandfather, Milos, was that Peter was just an infant when Peter's mother was raped and killed by the Croatians who were siding with the Germans during the First World War. Milos could not take care of Peter on his own, so as he found girlfriends, they became temporary mothers for Peter. It is safe to say Peter's life was negatively affected by war, uncertainty, family secrets, and religious hypocrisy and restraints. Perhaps these experiences formed his limited value on relationships with women. Peter was married five times, and I remember his wives in this way: wife number 1 was my mother, Vera; wife number 2 was the reason my parents divorced; wife number 3 was wonderful in my teenage eyes because she was not much older than me and she allowed me to do things my mother would not allow, like wear makeup and drive; wife number 4 was also named Vera, like my mother, who, in a moment of anger, signed her children away in a ready-made divorce paper Peter prepared before he deliberately made her upset; and wife number 5 was most likely as crazy as a loon; she might be his "comes around" in the saying "What goes around comes around."

Shortly after Peter's telephone call, he came to see me. In retrospect, the way they talked, I always thought he came to see Vera. It was obvious she never got over him—they looked so beautiful together. They were the same nationality, and they looked similar. I can remember thinking they were perfect together: she was beautiful, and he was handsome. What struck me the most was that they had the same crooked little smile, and their eyes sparkled whenever they reminisced about events and people in their past. As I matured and saw them together, I realized they were just emotional skeletons of their youth.

During the first visit, Peter took me shopping and bought me clothes and shoes I could only dreamed about before. It was arranged that I would visit him, and I did. Being too old to be a jockey, he was now a race horse breeder and trainer living on a most beautiful horse ranch. I was taken in by the wealth and freedom I felt there as opposed to the stifling, tension-filled environment in Vera's house.

At that time, Peter was married, for the third time, to a German woman. They were married so briefly I cannot recall her name. She was half his age, about twenty-five years old, and close enough to mine that I felt like she was a girlfriend I did not have. She allowed me to wear makeup, have nail polish, and occasionally drive her car, none of which was possible in my mother's house. Only whores wore make up and nail polish, Vera would say. I was taken in by her kindness. I called my mother to tell her I wanted to live with Peter. Per my mother, while Peter was telling me this was acceptable, he was calling Vera, pleading for her to say no to my desire to live with him. The way I looked at it when I thought about it, he did not want responsibility, and Vera couldn't lose her babysitter and lifeline.

In the 1960s, households had telephones with extensions, whereby one person could be talking and another person could be listening on the extension telephone, which was what Roy did. Within minutes of a telephone call with Peter, a terrible fight would ensue, and as usual, Roy used his fist instead of words. Such was the outcome more than once when Peter called. Peter often talked to Vera with intimate language. I did not know this until I picked up the telephone and heard him. I chastised him and told him what happened with Roy after he hung up. He promised to curtail his conversations, but because he was a selfish man, he rarely did.

His presence in our lives wreaked havoc in Vera's life. I got over him as a father shortly after a couple of visits. I don't know why she accepted his conversations or why he called periodically. He had not called for a couple of years, then, out of nowhere, we heard from him. It was so obvious, even as a child; I could see he was bad news. Sadly, she would or could never accept that premise.

A few years after the German wife left him, Peter moved from Ohio to San Bernardino, California. He sent me a ticket to visit him once, and there I met his fourth wife, Vera. Can you imagine? The same name as wife number 1, my mother. I have exclamations and bad words when I think of this situation. She was pregnant with a son. He named this son Dragan. Can you imagine? It was the same name as the illegitimate son he left in Serbia, whose mother caused my mother's divorce. Sometime after this visit, he and his fourth wife moved to Oxford, Michigan, to another lovely race horse farm. By the time I visited Peter the next time, he had a second child with Vera, a daughter, Barbara.

Ten years later, after his divorce from Vera, his ego insisted in telling me how cleverly he divorced this wife. Keep in mind that this father—I use the term loosely—is telling this story to me, his married daughter with two children of her own. In a word, he was and still is gross. He started off with telling me he was moving to New Jersey and was looking for a home. He met a realtor and fell in love instantly. Immediately after this meeting, he convinced this woman to travel with him to Croatia, where he owned a home, and per both of their stories, he left her there for a month while he sorted out his fourth marriage, or I should say, divorce. He continued, upon his return from Croatia, he went to his lawyer and drew up his divorce papers. He told Vera he was taking all the cash to the bank and the jewelry to the bank safe. He knew Vera was a French woman with a hot temper, and he knew how to push her buttons. So he did. He made her angry, she threatened divorce, he pulled out the divorce paper, and in her anger, she signed the paper. In the divorce papers, she signed over everything, including their home and children. Now, Peter, Mr. Selfish, had a girlfriend in Croatia who, by the way, per her admission, was a newlywed. Peter had two small children: a son, aged nine, and a daughter, aged seven, same age as my first daughter, Raquel. There is a lot to be said about men and women like Peter and his new wife, but why take time to use bad language? The owners of the horse farm were kind but older people, and they could not help with the children's care.

Peter pitted the children against their mother. They wanted nothing to do with her, and their mother was devastated. At the end of his story, Peter painted a desperate picture of not having anyone to care for Barbara. Because my daughter was the same age, I decided to keep Barbara until he could make other arrangements. After a year, he uprooted Barbara. Ultimately, in her teens, she left home and fell into rash and unproductive activities, too often a logical progression when children do not have steady homes and love.

You will recognize this pattern and outcome when I tell you about my marriage and divorce. You will surely exclaim, "My goodness, she married a replica of Peter!"

Severing Ties with Toxic Peter

As you have probably deducted by now, I was now married and have children at this point. So Peter would have no reason to call my mother, Vera. But he did, which led me back to my earlier conclusion that Peter and Vera could never let go of each other. That would stay their burden and secret until she died.

Unknown to me, he continued to call Vera until Peter's wife and Roy's jealousy got the best of all of them. I knew nothing about the circus they created among themselves until one day, I received a call from Peter's loony wife with nasty language and threats that if I didn't stop calling their house, I would be arrested, and hung up. I had just returned from an out-of-town trip, and I was shocked, to say the very least. I called her back and asked what was happening and tried to tell her I had not talked to Peter for some time. She wouldn't listen to anything I was saying, just returned to cursing and telling me I would go to jail if I called again. I was beside myself. I got into my car and drove to my father's house in Ocala, Florida, a one-hour-and-a-half drive. I knocked on the door, and Peter's daughter Barbara answered and informed me that I could not come in. At the same time, in the background I could hear Peter's wife yelling, "Tell her to leave or I will call the police!"

Most likely based on our past relationship, Barbara listened to my parental tone and let me in. Peter's wife ran to her bedroom and locked the door like a scared child. Just to give the reader a visual or a perspective, I am five feet tall and weigh a hundred pounds. I was shocked at her behavior. I talked with her through the door, but she was relentless about calling the police. I said, "Okay, but I want to know what is happening." She proceeded to tell me that my mother told her I made the last call to her with bad language and threats. Oh mercy, suddenly, it all made sense. Roy called Peter and threatened him not to call the house again, and Kitty, or whatever his current's wife's name was, called Vera to tell her not to call her house. Once I put the story together, I returned home, never to discuss this matter with either couple again, because it was too painful and would serve no purpose.

This event, like no other, made it clear how treacherous Peter was. That he was always in for himself no matter who got hurt.

By Marrying Roy, Vera Jumped Out of Peter's Frying Pan into Roy's Fire

After the death of my grandmother, Vera was often in despair. She blamed herself for writing the letter. She blamed Roy for bringing his mother to the States first and the havoc his mother caused. She was consumed with guilt and blame. She hated herself, and she hated Roy. The first divorce had affected her so profoundly it ruined her life, so much so that she would fear another divorce so intensely she would live with Roy's abuse for the rest of her life, in great pain, turmoil, and sacrifice to herself and her children.

For many years, I begged her to leave. But she never did.

I am not sure if Peter took advantage of her loneliness or if their conversations shone a light on their mutual loneliness. Perhaps both. After all, only they could bring back some fond, innocent memories. They had their loss and love for Rosa, my grandmother, to talk about. They loved her, and she loved them. They shared many friends from their youth; in fact, Peter sent one of their mutual childhood friends to represent him at Vera's funeral.

I've heard it said that the heart never lets go of the first love it experiences. Sadly, I believe that was true in their case.

I did not see my father, Peter, for many years after the unpleasant event, until we accidentally ran into each other in Serbia, at the horse races, the year my mother died. I was with my brother Dusan. He saw us and did not acknowledge us. I gave the waiter $100 to approach him with a beer and tell him his daughter bought him a beer and was sitting at the ring-side table, waiting for him. He feared his wife might make a scene, so he took her home and returned to acknowledge me. Life is a mystery! It was, and still is, a mystery to me how we met by chance in this one moment, place, and time in Serbia, yet we lived only ninety minutes from each other in Florida and never ran into each other intentionally or otherwise. Perhaps this meeting was arranged by divine intervention, perhaps by the intense emotions I felt when I saw him, knowing my meeting with him was to result in saying goodbye to him as I did to my mother, Vera, and all the people I loved and lost.

As I spotted my father walking toward me, I felt a subtle, intense, luminous radiation surrounding me. I've never experienced such a feeling since. I could see myself and all the strangers at the track suspended, standing still, frozen in one most enjoyable moment in my childhood. While I was in that state, I was observing my paternal grandfather, Milos, walking toward me with his eyes on his program, like he used to do when I was a child. I was overjoyed. Right behind him, I saw my handsome uncle walking next to my mother. I noted she was smiling like she did when she was young. His hair and mustache were jet-black, as when he was a younger man. I wanted to run to them, but I was suspended, and I was able to observe only. I saw my sweet grandmother carrying her race program, folded in half, walking toward the racetrack fence, with her reading glasses placed halfway down her nose, looking at me, smiling with that gentle smile. I saw my father as a young man, in his jockey outfit, walking his horse toward the starting line. The aura of their presence felt so real it was captured in my heart and mind as real as a movie. Each time I think of that moment, I wonder if they all assembled in that one moment to ease my pain by letting me know they were together once again after their death, or if my spirit somehow conjured up this vision and feeling to ease my pain of losing all of them. The human spirit cannot be tamed.

While I was basking in the moment, my father spoke and hugged me hello. The moment was gone. I have never experienced such an eerie feeling again.

Junior High School

After my grandmother's death, my mother immersed herself in work, and I immersed myself in school. Somehow, we both knew we were now each other's only lifeline. There was no turning back and no help forthcoming.

I had been in the United States for only three years. Vera knew school was hard for me as it related to English. She began to worry that I might not be able to graduate high school in four years. She knew I could not go to summer school, for I must watch the children during summer. She began to stress me out. I must not embarrass her, she said. I must do everything I could to pass in school. Meanwhile, I was struggling because the subjects were more complicated in seventh grade.

I was lucky. Once again, I think God was looking after me. I met my seventh-grade teacher, Mrs. Whitethorn, may God bless her, wherever she is in heaven. She saw a nervous little girl who spoke with very broken English, and I saw a sweet smile and felt a gentle hand on my shoulder as I struggled to tell her about myself. I was comforted because she was much like my sixth-grade teacher, Ms. Freedman. Mrs. Whitehorn was a caring and supportive soul. She comprehended my situation, that it was virtually impossible for me to complete seventh grade without extra help. She prepared a plan and asked me to set my sights on schoolwork during school, after school, and on the weekends. And that was what I proceeded to do. Mrs. Whitehorn arranged with other teachers to help me. Daily I would spend an hour in first grade, one hour in second grade, and one hour in third grade to learn English structure, sounds, writing, and the remainder of the day, I would return to seventh grade for all other subjects. In the evenings and weekends, Mrs. Whitehorn arranged for Mrs. Brown, the English teacher, and her college daughter to work on writing and reading with me. I was progressing rapidly, and I graduated from junior high school. I was blessed.

We should sing teachers praises because they can truly make the difference between failure and success in a child's life.

At this juncture, I began to feel hope. I reaffirmed to myself that God was really looking after me by sending me help. I was feeling less alone in my belief that there were kind people all around me. From this point on, I knew I walked alone, but I didn't panic, because my belief in God propelled me forward as I continued my journey.

Taking Care of Zoran and Zorica

After eighth grade, we moved from Elmhurst to Villa Park, a suburb literally on the other side of the track from the affluent Elmhurst. Villa Park was a less-affluent area, but our house was bigger, three bedrooms. In Elmhurst, we lived in a two-bedroom house where all three of us children lived in one bedroom. I was excited. I had a less-crowded bedroom. I even got a radio in my room, the first perk I ever got. I shared my room with Zorica. She was a sweet girl, and she was five years old then. I was pretty much her joint caretaker ever since she was six months old.

At the end of my eight-grade school year, I was told I would have to watch Zoran and Zorica during summer vacations from school. In my mother's eyes and Roy's needling, I had to earn my keep. To earn my keep, I was to watch the children during summer, make dinner promptly at five o'clock before Roy and my mother came home, clean house, and do the washing. It was now that I realized I was a stepchild to Roy and that I was brought to this country to help Vera, not be her child. I understood Cinderella.

At this juncture, things continued to get more complicated. I was embarking on normal teenage confusion and fear of beginning high school without my mentors, Ms. Freedman and Mrs. Whitehorn.

Before I discuss watching Zoran and Zorica, I will need to discuss Zoran. As I wrote, with intense help from schoolteachers, I was now speaking English reasonably well, although with an accent. Roy was not an engaging person, and until his death, he never spoke or wrote much English. Vera was advancing, but working in a factory, she did not get much interaction with people; thus, her English was limited. So when the children, Zoran or Zorica, had problems or needs in school, I would always have to go with my mother to interpret. The year before I was to watch the children during the summer, Zoran's teacher requested to see our mother. During this meeting, the teacher recommended that my parents seek psychological assistance for Zoran. The teacher felt Zoran was displaying problems in focusing and following directions. My mother wanted to seek assistance; however, Roy was stuck in the old-fashioned thinking. He felt Vera spoiled Zoran and he just needed discipline. His usual blame game. He refused to consider counseling because, in his view, this would be an embarrassment to his family. I was too young to know any different, but now I can see the gross error in his judgment. Roy's nephew was diagnosed with obsessive-compulsive disorder; thus, there was a possibility of inherited issues in his family. Roy elected to ignore the suggestions from the teachers, and instead, he proceeded to degrade and discipline Zoran, which ultimately resulted in Zoran's quitting school and leaving home at the age of sixteen. He struggled all his life, and he died from a drug overdose in the back seat of a police car in his late thirties. This should give the reader an idea how challenging it was for a fourteen-year-old girl to watch a troubled seven-year-old Zoran. He should have never been cared for by a worrying, inexperienced fourteen-year-old girl. Zoran was a troubled but otherwise gentle boy and man. He used drugs and liquor to solve what was ailing him. Through the mixture of drugs and his father's example, he gradually moved to occasionally physically abusing his girlfriends. After his death, Zorica and I went to clean Zoran's apartment, and we were stunned with what we found. We found all his beds without sheets and all his clothes on the floor of his closet. His nightstand drawers were full of cigarette ashes, his dresser drawers were full of empty cigarette boxes, and the kitchen counters were lined with empty rum gallon bottles. The last year of his life, he called me in the middle of the night to tell me gypsies were removing his furniture. Upon his death, his father described Zoran as stupid and spoiled by his mother instead of being an ill or troubled man.

Based on my education and experience, I know that if a child has psychological problems, the problems become apparent, in some form, in kindergarten or first grade because this is when a child must navigate to achieve learning skills within measurable standards. It is my suggestion that all parents and teachers acknowledge problems and seek help for the child immediately rather than label the child as a disciplinary problem. It most surely can mean the difference between life and death or, at a minimum, the difference between a troubled and peaceful life. My brother Zoran is a perfect example for this statement.

Taking care of Zorica was not as challenging as watching Zoran. Taking care of Zoran was extremely hard for him and me. He could not accept directions, and he could not exercise self-control. For example, if I was upstairs, he would leave the house through the basement door. Our parents would find out from neighbors, and we would get yelled at and, at times, beaten. At this stage of my development, I was trying to solve my own developmental stage of intimacy versus isolation. I was a teenager then. I was not skilled enough to teach him self-control or information processing.

Anyone who has raised children knows this was not just a summer job; it was the job of raising two small children, mischievous, later-diagnosed-troubled five-year-old Zoran and sweet three-year-old Zorica.

What did I know about raising children day in and day out? I was only fourteen years old, struggling with my own teen confusion. I was isolated. I was not allowed to have friends over. In later years, I found out this was because my stepfather was a gross man, and for that reason, my mother did not trust him with me or my girlfriends. I vouch for her opinion here; he was a grossly unkind man.

During my brief few years in my mother's troubled household, I developed traits that caused me to worry about everything and everyone every day. I perfected this defeating system of living during my high school years. I had been working for years to manage these traits once I realized they were not sustainable.

After the stress of watching the small children all summer and toward the end of my first year in high school, I began to revert to breaking out with welts from my nervousness as I did when I first arrived in the United States. The same doctor treated my new breakout. Once again, I received shots to cure the welts. But there were no shots to ease the tension in the household.

To this day, I must work diligently to manage this impulse to worry, especially over things that are out of my control. From my personal experience, working as care manager for abused and neglected children, and my studies in psychology, I believe pressure cooker households wreak havoc on a child's life, havoc that stays with them, to some degree, all the days of their lives.

Preparing for High School

I was stewing with worry. I knew I needed summer school help, but I was to watch the children all summer. I felt lonely, especially when I saw my neighbors Richie and Dennis on the west side of the yard, having fun with my neighbor Denise and her girlfriends. They invited me to join them, but my mother did not allow it—she labeled Denise a whore because she could hang around with boys while her mother was at work. I was sad because when Denise talked to me over the fence, she seemed kind and felt sorry for me, I could tell. She and Richie were kind to me all through high school even though my mother was not nice to them.

It is good to teach our children to be kind to one another. Peer kindness is a wonderful cushion for children.

Dragana with half-brother Zoran and half-sister Zorica shortly after her arrival in the United States.

CHAPTER FOUR

CHILDHOOD IN AMERICA
High School, 1961–1966

By the age of sixty-nine, one would not think high school is necessarily a significant time in a person's life. In my case, high school years were the most significant. Some people and events in high school profoundly affected the rest of my life. Some enriched my life, while others almost destroyed it. Some people experience good parenting and having strong families, while others, like me, do not. And when you do not have good parenting and a strong extended family, you are apt to flounder and let others take you where they will when you should have sat still and let God carry you where he will. I am that person who did not have supportive, peaceful parenting; thus, the decisions I made and the experiences I encountered during my high school years were significant enough to affect most of my entire life.

Freshman

I lived in Villa Park then, so by designation, I should be going to Willowbrook High School. However, Willowbrook was a newly built high school, not yet finished to receive my class;

thus, we were bussed to the more affluent York High School in Elmhurst.

I was excited and scared at the same time. My experiences with teachers and peers in fourth through eighth grades were positive and comforting because Ms. Freedman and Mrs. Whitehorn were very supportive and they motivated the students to be helpful to me. I basked in their approval each time I made progress in my schoolwork. I believe this experience is the reason I am a willing and effective mentor to young people.

I am a proponent of teachers pairing up students in the classroom. This idea promotes goodwill among the students, resulting in greater knowledge sharing and support for one another. To do nothing promotes bullying.

As I started school, I took each class seriously. I was attentive, I took notes, I read and reread everything, but comprehension was slowing me down. I understood the subject matter, but I couldn't do well on the exams. I was struggling, just barely making Cs and Ds.

Meanwhile, on a positive note, I was pleased my peers voted me into the student council. I did well there but had to resign because I could not make the required grade point average. I felt bad that I no longer belonged to a group. I felt comfortable in a group. But then as I found out in later years, who doesn't seek to belong to a group? That is why cliques are formed. Mercy.

I didn't let this setback deter me. I took home all my books to study every evening. I always had my four-inch *Webster's Dictionary* with me to help me understand what I was reading, and of course, in those days, 1961–1966, we all wore gym suits and sneakers, so we had to carry them home for washing. Believe me, it was a full load, especially for a short five-foot-tall skinny girl like me. Oh, and by the way, we did not have the nice back packs we have nowadays.

The Beginning of the Demise of All My Dreams

One day, I was boarding the school bus rather late. Once on the bus, I had to hurry to find a seat. I could hear the bus driver closing the door, which signaled he would be starting to drive right away. As I described in the previous paragraph, I always carried a full load. If the bus started before I sat down, my books, dictionary, gym suit and shoes, and purse, would be strewn all over the floor. I knew I had to scramble to find the first available seat. As normal buses go, each seat was big enough for two students. I started to sit in the first available seat I noticed. Just as I started to sit down, the guy who was already in the seat by the window ordered me to sit in the seat behind him. I wasn't embarrassed as much, as I thought, *What a rude guy.* But because I was rushed and overloaded, I did not argue. In those days, I was very shy and quiet because of my English and lack of experience in dealing with peers outside of the class- room. Trust me, I am no longer shy. This guy was Ed, who was to ultimately devour thirty-one years of my life.

It turned out I sat next to Tommy, a very kind and sweet boy, who also happened to be Ed's friend. He tried to explain Ed to me. Really, to date, there is no explanation for a creature like Ed, any more than there is an explanation for a creature like my father, Peter. Only to say that they are creatures that suck the life out of others with their lies and manipulation. Who knew guys like that existed? Obviously, my mother did, and if I lis- tened to her sad stories, I would have known about these types of guys. But I did not listen to my yesterday's woman, who had already been on a journey with a guy like Ed, my father, Peter.

Tommy told me Ed was a broad jumper in track and that day, as he jumped during practice, he dug his shoe cleat into his hand, which explained why I never saw the rude guy on the bus before. Usually, he was at practice after school. Dumb ass.

I don't know when it started that Ed, the big guy on campus, began to pursue me, but pursue me he did. I did not like him very much. I tried to avoid him. One day, he came to my house, and my mother made it very clear to him that I was not allowed to hang around with boys and shooed him away. When Ed left, she went on one of her angry rants, making it clear that he was not to hang around me. Ed was a persistent guy, and so saying no to Ed was like waving a red flag in front of a bull. This is still true about him. Off and on he would weave in and out of my life. He would show up wherever I was. I lived in fear; if my mother found out, I would be humiliated right on the spot, as was her usual approach. I had received more than one punishment over Ed.

To this day I have a real problem tolerating someone embarrassing someone else. That fear is horrible because you constantly live in anticipation of a negative outcome. In other words, you always wait for the other shoe to drop. I think the parents who rant and rave prepare their children to be obedient out of fear, so when the children encounter a person who is yelling and ranting, they automatically take the obedient stance. Anyway, that, I think, was what made me put up with the angry bird in Ed's disposition.

When he would follow me around and encounter my friends, if he got jealous, he would yell and carry on, and I would freeze with fear and embarrassment just as I did when my mother yelled. Just for the record, I no longer tolerate anyone yelling or ranting at me or anyone else in my presence. Being yelled at is degrading and abusive.

Dear reader, if you are constantly yelled at, require the person that is yelling and ranting at you to stop. Yelling is the initial step in control by fear and embarrassment. If the person will not stop, exclude him/her from your life before you lose all your power. If you take no action, he/she will advance to the next steps, like rage and push and shove and possibly worse.

Melinda and Her Family

My freshman year in high school (1961–1962) was also the time when Russians were threatening to bomb America, and families that could were creating underground bomb shelters. I never knew of such shelters until the subject came up in class.

One day, while we were discussing bomb shelters, a girl invited me to come to her house, asking if I wanted to see a bomb shelter. Mercy, I wanted to see that. This girl's name was Melinda. From that day on, Melinda and I became lifelong friends. I am happy we've remained friends. I am particularly grateful she was my friend during my high school years. I mentioned in previous texts that my mother did not allow me to invite friends to the house, boy or girl. She also fiercely refused to let me go to other people's houses, and one can easily imagine what that was like for a teenager. The isolation was at times unbearable. Schoolbooks helped pass the time but did nothing to build a person's confidence or mellow life as it marched on. I begged and pleaded for my mother to let me go, and after much pleading, my mother called Melinda's mother, Mrs. Finney. Mrs. Finney was like Mrs. Freedman and Mrs. Whitehorn, kind and gentle, soft-spoken, always smiling. I grew to love her like my own mother, and I still do to this day.

Yes, indeed, they did have a bomb shelter.

I also met Mr. Finney, who was the opposite of Mrs. Finney. He was a kind but stern preacher man. The next time I wanted to hang out with Melinda, my mother talked with Mr. Finney. I was glad, because I knew he was much like my mother. When they were done talking, my mother thought he was as stern as she was, and subsequently, I was allowed to go to Melinda's house often. What my mother never knew was that Mr. Finney was a reasonable man who understood the principles of keeping your kids and their friends within earshot, as the saying goes. Mr. Finney allowed Melinda and her friends to hang out in the basement to listen to music, talk, and dance, with the condition that the kitchen door leading to the basement stayed open and everyone cleared out by 9:00 p.m. Occasionally, Mr. Finney would do spot checks, as we called them. He would just pop down the stairs to see how everyone was doing. Funny, later, when I had teenagers, I modeled some of Mr. Finney's techniques.

I was to go straight home after school, pick up Zoran and Zorica, and make dinner before Vera came home from work. Roy and Vera's endless tension continued. I hid in my bedroom as much as I could, I did homework, and I helped the little kids with theirs.

I was struggling to pass freshman year, and by the good graces of the teachers and a couple of helpful peers, I pass ninth grade.

At the end of the freshman year, Willowbrook was ready to receive the Villa Park students. Melinda and I moved to Willowbrook, while Ed stayed at York High School. After all, how could he leave? He was the jock on campus. Mercy me. I was glad to transfer and leave Ed behind, or so I thought.

Once I met Ed, he was like a snake lost in your house; you don't see it, but you know it's there, and it comes out whenever it wants.

Sophomore Year

Looking back on high school years at the age of sixty-nine is like looking into the rearview mirror; some things I see clearly, and other things are blurry. This is particularly true of my high school years. I believe we remember years by the events and people we meet that make some sort of mark on our hearts.

I can't remember clearly how it came about that Ed started to pursue me sophomore year, but he did. Wherever I went, he seemed to be there. About midyear, he came to my house in the middle of winter, in snow and slush, wearing light shoes and a summer jacket. He looked frozen. My mother felt sorry for him and let him stay at the house. I heard it said that once you feed a cat, it always comes back. As an analogy, that was what happened with Ed. He totally built trust with my mother, Zoran, and Zorica. She let her guard down and allowed him to start coming over to our house. Up to this point, I used her as my shield not to encourage him to follow me around. When he would come over, he and my mother and I would play cards. I think my mother felt sorry for him, and ultimately, she treated him like a son. He was a distraction in our stress-filled household. He could turn on the charm, and he started calling my mother Ma. Oh dear, that was too close.

Through many setbacks, which I will not discuss because that's their story, Ed's family was not set well financially. He had to contribute to buying his own clothes, for example. I identified with that because I had to do the same thing. By now I was working at Sears part-time after school to pay for my needs, like winter coats, clothes, books, etc. He was an athlete, so going to school and training created a challenge for him to find hours to work. One year, my mother helped me buy him a new pair of track shoes. Another year, I saved and bought him his letterman jacket. And so on. Slowly Ed endeared himself to me and my mother. The lesson here is, don't assume a snake is not deadly just because its tail is not rattling.

While I was watching the children during the summer, Ed's coming over was strictly forbidden. Both Ed and I feared Vera's wrath. He was present at one of Roy and Vera's push-and-shove events, so he knew things could get ugly very fast in my household. Sneaking was not an option because we knew Zoran or

Zorica were little and would slip and let it out of the bag. I was glad, because I was uncomfortable with his trying to advance passion with too much inappropriate touching during kissing.

I was Sixteen Then

By old Serbian standards, it was time for a girl-child to prepare for marriage. Serbian parents would then begin looking for suitable prospects. Thank goodness this has changed somewhat nowadays.

My mother decided early on that Ed was not suitable to be considered as a marriage match. He was not cultured, he was not from a well-to-do family, he was not Serbian, and he was not Serbian Eastern Orthodox. She viewed Ed more as a son than a suitor for her daughter. She also saw through his charm. She saw Peter in Ed. She would tell me this many years later. Because she viewed him as a son, she let him hang around our house every so often. I don't think Ed and I viewed his visits the same way my mother did.

At this juncture, it is appropriate to bring back the subject of the dreaded Serbian social traditions, mores, and religious constraints in the 1960s. It was obvious my mother wanted to overcorrect what happened to her, and by the end of the summer, she had a good wind in her sails. Suddenly, it was okay for me to go on a formal date with a young man who was in college studying engineering, was a Serbian Eastern Orthodox, and was out of a family in good social and financial standing. I tried to go along with it a couple of times; however, at this time of my life, I couldn't bear the idea of ever marrying, let alone marrying a Serbian man. I associated wife-beating with a Serbian husband.

Another subject my mother harped on was virginity. Days in and days out, every time the conversation of going out with friends arose, the virginity subject came about, and here is how it went: If you are not a virgin, no good man will ever want you. You will be forced to marry the person who ruined you. I was convinced this was true. I did not know any better. Later in life, when I reflected on high school years with friends, I was amazed and distraught at how totally naive and unenlightened I was about so many things that were necessary and natural to know during those developmental years.

Junior Year: A Life-Altering Event

I don't know exactly when it happened, but sometime in my junior year of high school, although guarded, Vera let up a little on my seeing Ed. I also don't know when I started to like Ed. I started to like him, but I was always on guard not to get too involved. He was too volatile, and I knew he would go away to college. I longed to find my brother and sisters, and the best way I could figure out to do that was for me to go to airline college and get a job with the airlines. I was dead set to go to work for the airlines. No matter what, I had a plan to leave home as soon as possible.

I liked spending time with Ed's family; it got me out and away from my family. His sister and brother-in-law were wonderful people, and his brothers, his stepfather, and even his mother warmed up to me. We would go out with friends, but most of the time, we would spend time with his family. Occasionally, we would park and smooch underneath the weeping willow tree located in his parent's backyard. Everybody let down their guard, me included.

But toward the end of the year, I started to lose interest in being around Ed. I was beginning to feel threatened by his jealousy. If I was in a group, he would show up and make embarrassing scenes. Rumors came back to me that suggested he was a cheater. But the less I wanted to see him, the more intense he became. If I was in a car with another male friend, he would chase down the car. He and his buddies would intimidate guys who asked me out. *Nasty.* Sometime toward the end of our junior school year, he asked me to come over to his house for dinner. As I said previously, my mother had let up, but she was still vigilant. My mother talked to his mother to make sure we were not going to be home alone. His mother assured my mother she would be home. I don't know how it came about, but his mother left the house. We were alone. I didn't think much about it because I never imagined what was about to happen.

We were sitting on Ed's bed, as we often did, talking, occasionally kissing. Suddenly, one minute we were kissing, and the next minute, Ed became aggressive. As I was struggling to pull away, he held me down, and before I knew it, I felt his privates in me. In minutes, the struggle was over. I was bleeding. I did not know that this was what virginity was about. I had never seen a man's private parts before, and the act of sexual intercourse had never crossed my mind. *Never.* I was very naive. In my family, we never talked about sexual activity. In 1964, we did not see nudity, sexual acts, or porn on television or in school. The only thing my mother harped on was virginity and how I would be ruined if I lost it before marriage. I was devastated, I was frightened, and I had no one to talk to about what just happened. I went home in a panic. I knew very little about how one gets pregnant. I rolled everything in one statement: if you have sex, you will lose your virginity, and if you lose your virginity, no good man will want you, and you will get pregnant. I laid in my bed, in the silence of my bedroom, and all I could feel was this enormous terror. For days, I lived in guilt and fear and prayer. Finally, I got my menstrual cycle. I knew this signified I was not pregnant. I breathed with a sigh relief. I must have thanked God a million times. In fact, this was a pivotal point when I truly believed God was listening and was with me when I felt alone and isolated. At the same time, I was in despair over losing my virginity. I felt betrayed by Ed.

I have now known Ed for over fifty years, and I can still remember his aggression and my immediate sense of betrayal and intense fear.

After sorting things out, I did not want to see Ed again. Now that I realized Ed was reckless, that he did not care about consequences, my fear shifted from fear of losing my virginity to fear of getting pregnant. I tried avoiding him. But the more I ignored him, the more he pursued me. If I was going somewhere with another boy, he and his friends would try to run us off the road. They would stop and threaten any boy who dared to ask me out. It was horrible. Finally, at the end of my junior year of school, Ed latched on to someone else. I was relieved. I carried the burden of guilt and worry that no other man would want me through my senior year of high school, until I made another grave error to see Ed one more time.

Nowadays, this event is called date rape, as it should be. To guys like Ed, this act is something they do without any thought, yet it is a life-altering act for the girl.

My wish for the young girls, based on my experience, is to take time to search for a good man, not a good date. If they find that they have given up their virginity, I want them not to think they are a lesser person for the loss. In some ways, a woman's virginity is part of her power base—power of self-control, power of giving herself when she feels ready and to whom she feels is a worthy mate.

Senior Year

Once Ed found someone else, he left me alone. Once he was out of my scope, I started calming down. I worked hard on my schoolwork to make sure I graduated and on my part-time job to make as much money as I could for airline college and a car. I started my research on airline colleges because I had it in my head that I wanted to work for the airlines, and no other job would do. I knew I was too short to be a stewardess, but I also knew there were many other jobs in that business. I found an excellent twelve-week airline college program. The program suited me very well because it was split in two sessions, six weeks at home studies and six weeks in Kansas City, Missouri. The program afforded me opportunities to save for my out-of-town tuition while completing the first six weeks at home. In the Serbian culture, it was not acceptable for a single girl to leave home until she married, and that motivated me to attend an out-of-town educational institution. I knew I could not afford a four-year college, so airline college was the next best thing.

After losing my virginity, I was convinced I would never get married, and that was fine with me.

High school was a struggle for me with my English and my family, so graduation was a great relief and achievement. I can recall my thoughts like it was yesterday as I was putting on my graduation gown. I thought now I could get a job with the airlines and travel the world to find my family.

Dreaming is good, because dreams can keep you going, and if you keep going, dreams can come true.

What was your high school experience like?

What were your high school dreams?

CHAPTER FIVE

ELOPEMENT AND CONSEQUENCES, 1966–1973

We eloped. Oh my god, what did I do?

As usual, I was busy with watching Zoran and Zorica during the summer. There was a lot of conversation with friends about who was going to college and who was going to work. During one such conversation, I was told Ed was leaving for Miami. I talked to my mother about it, and she said we should give him a little going-away present. I purchased a little gift and arranged to meet him.

During our conversation, I fell back on my abandonment triggers when I realized he was leaving for Miami, and he realized he was leaving for Miami without much financial support. I really don't know why he asked me, "If I were to ask you to marry me right now, would you do it?" And I don't know why I said yes. I have gone over my answer a million times, and each time, I came up with the same answers. I didn't believe he meant the question just as I didn't really mean the answer. I didn't take time to analyze my answer at the time this conversation was going on; however, I know I didn't want to hurt his feelings by saying no, and I know I thought it was a safe answer because I didn't believe it could happen. In the first place, we were both underage, and Ed was leaving in a week. But it did happen! Everything was accelerated. We didn't have to wait two days for blood tests; the doctor squeezed us in. The jeweler engraved our rings within a few hours. The license office took us in the same day. We knew for sure my mother would not give us permission, so we avoided her. We knew Ed's mother would not go along with it, but Ed knew his stepfather would go along, and he did. Ed's brother-in-law went along with being the best man. A friend of mine was getting married, so it was prearranged that I would spend a night at her house, so when I told my mother I would be gone overnight, she did not question it. And two days from the meeting, we eloped. And we were married. We went on a one-night honeymoon, and two days later, Ed left for Miami, and a few weeks later, I left for Atlantic Airline College in Kansas City, Missouri.

Our meeting was a perfect collision. For over thirty years, I regretted making that call. I have pondered on what could have caused me to go through this event, especially since I did not even like the idea of getting married, ever. It was not until I completed my college degree in human development that I finally understood how my personal issue with abandonment contributed to my going through with the elopement. If you reference back to my traumatic departure from Serbia to America, you can see how departures like Ed's to Miami can trigger my abandonment issues. It is an issue I still struggle with.

Ed wrote almost every day. He discussed intimate matters and our marriage. I panicked and purchased a Lane Hope chest with a lock to hide away his letters so that my mother would not find them.

Meanwhile, in my mother's world, nothing changed. While I was in Kansas City, she called crying and screaming that Roy beat her again. She wanted me to talk with him to scare him again. I did just that. During that conversation, I felt relieved that I was married. In my warped view of the world, for a second, I saw being married to Ed as an opportunity to move out of my mother's home environment. Good Serbian girls did not move out of their parents' home until they were married. Ludicrous!

The longer I was away from home and Ed, the more the word *married* began to explode in my brain like a bullet shot. Not long after the conversation with my mother, I began to awaken to a realization that I was in a no-win situation. I began to panic with the realization that I was damned if I returned to my house and damned if I went with Ed. Intermittently, I would be nauseous because I was beginning to see that I did what my mother did when she married my father—jumped out of the frying pan into the fire. It seemed she married my father just as she turned sixteen years old because he lured her into losing her virginity. Grandfather and religious hypocrisy did the rest to convince her that with the loss of her virginity, she was worthless. Suddenly, I understood Vera's fears that I would do the same and follow in her footsteps. In a flash, I saw clearly that I fulfilled Vera's greatest fears.

I had excellent grades at the college. And then a wonderful break came my way. Braniff and American Airlines conducted job interviews just before graduation, and I was invited for one. I was very pleased with the overall experience and with myself.

I returned home immediately upon completion of the program. Almost at the same time, Ed decided he didn't like his track scholarship in Miami and returned to Villa Park to attend Elmhurst College on a football scholarship.

While in Kansas City, I had time to think objectively and on an adult level. Once I thought with clarity instead of emotion, I realized I did not want to be married. When I returned home to Villa Park, I was armed with the full understanding of what happened. I tried to tell my mother, but every time I approached her with the word *marriage*, she would go into angry panic, so I decided to keep quiet until I could afford an apartment and move out. I knew my mother well; she would do nothing less than disown me. That was the Serbian way—they would rather see their children suffer for breaking the rules than help them correct their mistakes. Well, that plan did not work out.

My mother was relentless. She continued to be out of sync with my life. I was almost twenty years old, graduated from airline college, had a temporary job in her factory as a file clerk, yet she still had some warped sense of the old Serbian rules that I needed to be home by ten o'clock. One evening, Ed came to pick me up for a date. I was not home yet. While he was waiting for me, my mother gave Ed a ten o'clock curfew time, and he wasn't going to have anyone tell him what to do. Beyond that, all I knew was, when I arrived home, all hell broke loose.

Ed blurred out that we were married. Within minutes, my mother gathered all my belongings and my hope chest and threw me and Ed out. The following Sunday, she went to our church priest and disowned me. She did not have anything to do with me for three years, until I gave birth to my first child.

By her reaction, it was apparent that she did not learn anything from her experience with Peter and her father. So I was left alone to fend for myself. Ed had his parents, sister, and brothers.

If I thought I went to hell when Vera pitched me out and went to the church priest to disown me, I was wrong. Vera's actions just propelled me to the doorway of hell. Ed's mother,

Betty, moved me in. When she found out the news, she acted just as crazy as my mother. And rightly so. Although she was not my favorite yesterday's woman, she knew where that road would lead us. She was left with raising three preschool children alone after her husband abandoned her.

Living in Ed's Mother's House

Well, there we were with my stuff and nowhere to go. After her rants, Ed's mother agreed to let us stay in Ed's bedroom.

For starters, by contrast, let me tell you how Vera and Betty maintained their homes. Granted, Vera had me to help. Her house was so spotless you could have eaten off her floors. Betty's house was exactly the opposite. Not to be critical, just to point out the abrupt change in my environment. When we washed clothes, we meticulously separated white clothes from colored, different materials, etc. Betty, bless her soul, washed her sheets, rugs, dishrags, and T-shirts all in one load of wash. That was just a little jolt, although not too worrisome. I knew I would wash my own clothes.

Ed's bedroom was small, with just a twin bed in the room. In that moment, I saw no options beyond this. I felt panic, intense fear, a feeling of drowning; I felt the helplessness an innocent person might feel when the prison doors lock as he protests his innocence.

The next day, Ed left for school. I was left with an angry mother-in-law. She was angry at me and Ed's stepfather, who signed for us to be able to get married. She was not mad at her precious football star; he was the victim. In Betty's eyes, Ed could do no wrong. His siblings and I accepted that, although later in life, even she could see Ed was mean to the core.

Every morning, beginning with the first morning, Betty would sit at the dining room table five feet away from Ed's bedroom door to have coffee with Perry, the stepfather. She would begin with "She"—referring to me—"is a money-hungry foreigner. She is going to ruin his life! He is going to lose his scholarship! Those foreigners just latch on to the Americans." Just as a point of reference, I was a dual citizen of the United States and Serbia. A barrage of insults. On and on she would go. To keep peace, the old man would just grunt and agree. I knew the old man remembered who asked him to sign the approval and who convinced him to sign it. I also knew he wouldn't dare point that out to Betty, especially since he had by now successfully diverted all of Betty's anger onto me. What would you do? I sat in Ed's bedroom and cried, praying to hear from American Airlines soon so I could go to work.

I started to clean Ed's closet to make room for my clothes. On the top shelf, I found a Bible. In the Bible, I found all kinds of love letters. Dear God, most of them from young girls, some stating they were ready, while others were not yet ready for sex. I immediately realized he took pleasure in taking young girls' virginity. I was sick. I became angry with myself for being so naive as to let myself walk into this snare—the rape, the marriage, the lack of confidence to tell him after college that I did not want to be married to him. All of it. His response to the letters was that those days were over. I shouldn't have read the letters. In his usual style, he borrowed the words from Sonny and Cher. "It ain't me, babe." Must be you. This was to be his mantra for the next twenty-seven years.

As I am writing this paragraph, I ask myself, what was my mantra? Mine was to outrun the huge bolder that was rolling down the hill behind me.

God was good. He heard me and answered my prayers! It must be God. I did not talk to anyone else about my fears, hopes, and dreams but him. Within the weeks of my moving in to Ed's bedroom, I received a call from American Airlines' human resource representative, who offered me a job as reservation agent with a starting date in four days. I couldn't stand still! I went from despair to elation in one minute. Within a split second of accepting American's job, I saw freedom. The salary was great, and within minutes, I was planning my escape from Betty's house and from Ed. I immediately got into my car and started looking for a one-bedroom apartment. I mean *immediately*. I found a wonderful one-bedroom on the third floor near the train I would have to take to work. American Airlines was located on LaSalle and Madison in Downtown Chicago. At this point, I didn't care where it was located; my dream to work for American Airlines was coming true.

My New Mantra

My head was reeling. I was thinking somebody in heaven must really like me. I graduated from high school, I completed airline college, I bought a little car, and now I got my dream job. I was thinking I had developed wings; I am flying out of despair and into a sunny future. This sequence of events awakened a powerful "I can do it" feeling within me. I could do anything I was willing to pray and work for, and this became my new mantra.

The landlord required one month's rent plus a deposit. I calculated and figured that between my small savings and my future salary, I could afford to move into the apartment in three weeks. Since I had no furniture, I asked the landlord if I could pay the deposit two weeks after I moved in. He understood my plight, and I had always appreciated his support and understanding since. In the three years I rented the place, I was never late with the rent. Next, I went to Lincoln Furniture, famous for one-price, three-room cheap but nice matching furniture. I found what I liked. I was calming down. Next morning, when Betty started with her "She'll make Ed work, he won't be able to go to school and do his sports, and he'll lose his scholarship," I just prayed and told myself that God was in charge, not Vera and Betty. And in charge he was. Promptly in two weeks, when I got my first paycheck, I took Ed to see the apartment and the furniture. I told him we would be moving in a few days, but if he preferred to stay with his family, that would be okay with me.

Hindsight

In hindsight, I should have just moved in and moved on without Ed as useless baggage. But Ed was a good actor, some might say sociopath. He could cry, beg, plead, promise anything on a moment's notice, right on cue, knowing he had no intention of living up to anything. Being a naive sap, I fell for his act that time and many more in the twenty-seven years to follow, always thinking the next time would be different. As I will soon reveal, Ed never changed—only I did.

The first few months were peaceful. I went to work on the 5:15 a.m. train, and Ed went to school, practiced sports, and did part-time work. Or so I thought. Ed's lies were his way of life. My first inkling that something was wrong was when Ed called me to come to the police station with money for bail. Really, where was that money supposed to come from? I did as he asked. Being tight for the month's bills, I worked hours of overtime to cover his bail money. After a couple of these events, I refused to bail him out because I did not have the money and did not want to be delinquent with the bills. Next, he played his brother-in-law, Fred, when he fell into one of his follies. When his sister found out what was happening, she put a stop to it. Or at least she thought. But Fred, being a good person, continued to bail Ed out of one jam after another. Mercy, all the warning signs were there, that it was time to sever my ties with Ed, but I didn't act on them. He promised he would work harder to correct everything. No, he didn't; he just hid things better and lied more often.

In Ed's junior year in college, we decided to try to have a baby, which happened right away. I know now that this was a wrong but typical thing people do when they are drowning in their marriage. Things seemed to be going well. We named the baby girl Raquel. She was a sweet, easy baby. I adored her. She brought love into my heart, and she still does. It seemed we were making progress. I returned to work after three months. My mother-in-law needed the money, so we paid her to watch the baby. After a while, we asked my sister-in-law, Pam, to watch Raquel because of Betty's poor health.

Hindsight

Oh, my goodness! If he wasn't fulfilling his basic responsibilities, how did I think he would carry his weight after a child added more responsibilities? And he didn't. He was the guy who lost his two-year-old daughter at a ballpark.

Ed was settled at Elmhurst College. He was quite the star. Newspapers loved him. Apparently, so did his girlfriend. In our fourth year of marriage, I found out my husband had a girlfriend. He preferred I didn't go to his football games, and he tried to feed me some cow manure to make me believe he got nervous when the baby and I were at the games. Note to self: he was not nervous the year before. He denied. He denied, of course. He was an expert liar and denier by then, so along with denials, he always pleaded he loved me and Raquel only. By then, I had come a long way. I was more calculating than hurt or angry. I realized another similarity between my mother's life and mine beyond the virginity event. I was married to Ed, a liar and a cheater, and she was married to Peter, a liar and cheater. Wasn't that joyful?

Hindsight

I realize now that once the first batch of lies or the first sexual indiscretion event fell on me, I was never the same. At the very least, I was always on the lookout for the next. I was always doubting my senses. There was nowhere to hide from the betrayal of a cheating partner. Betrayal does not stop just because you stay and live on promises that it will not occur again; it stops when you leave the environment where betrayal lives.

From the very first plan I implemented successfully—that is, to go to airline college—I knew I had a good mind and strong will. I solidified this confidence when I implemented the plan that moved us in our first apartment. As soon as I implemented one plan successfully, I began preparing the next plan. I am still like that today. It kept me from panicking and stagnation. My new plan was to purchase a house.

From the very first paycheck, I had American Airlines payroll department deduct a few dollars from my paycheck and deposit half of the fund into my savings account and the other half toward purchasing American Airlines stock. I rode the train to work every day, so while riding, I read the newspaper and tracked American stocks. I calculated that in four years, I would have enough money for a down payment to purchase a house. I learned I could purchase a new home for less than an older established home, that it would go up in value faster, and all new appliance would be included. Mercy, how much more can you ask for? To ensure that I reached my goal, I also worked as much overtime as I could and every holiday for double time and a half-pay. This was my plan, and I worked it for four years. I am smiling as I write this paragraph. It worked!

Four years after we moved into our first apartment, I was ready to implement my new, ambitious plan: purchase a house.

I had a friend at American Airlines who was purchasing a new house in Lombard. We were familiar with the area. Lombard was a nice small town. We went to look at the houses, and we fell in love with a beautiful four-bedroom house. Financially, it was a little tight, so I prepared my argument for the builder. Between give and take a little on both sides, I could close on the home by the month's end. Also, Ed was to graduate in a few months, which meant he would take on a full-time job. Goodness, the subdivision and the house were so new we didn't even have sidewalks! We had to walk on planks. But that didn't matter. We owned a house.

Meanwhile, Ed, on the other hand, never had a plan—that I knew of, anyway. He just did exactly what he wanted regardless of the consequences. He never contributed a dime to the household until he found a full-time job. He claimed he worked part-time, and maybe he did, but he couldn't prove it by me. He used what he earned to maintain his big-jock-on-campus image. Pitiful, but true.

Shortly after we moved in to our house, I had a miscarriage. The doctors informed me during the cleaning that, most likely, I would not have any more children. All things considered, I thought that was acceptable to me under my circumstances.

The first year, we settled into our new house. Things were looking up. I got a promotion, which took a little pressure off the finances. Raquel started school. She was a sweet little girl, and everybody loved her sweet disposition and bright-yellow hair. Ed was Ed. There was no such thing as sitting down like a married couple, reviewing finances, planning vacations, and sharing ideas. When Ed left our house, no one ever knew where he was or what he was doing. This was to be true for twenty-seven years. He was always independent, until something gross he did fell on us both, which seemed to happen every year.

Like all fools, I kept thinking any day soon, he would wake up and see that he had responsibilities.

Hindsight

When I was young, an older woman, a yesterday's woman, once said to me, "Always have a plan of your own and always have a little savings account in your name. If your marriage lasts thirty years, use it for a nice vacation. If it fails, you will have a safety net." I should have listened to that Yesterday's Woman. She knew marriage could go either way.

Just when I started thinking I was moving toward the exit door out of hell, I once again found myself standing in front of the devil. Just when I felt things were settling down, I got a telephone call from some female telling me about my husband's dalliances. As I hung up the telephone, I could hear my heart pounding. I became weak in the knees. I confronted him, and as always, I got lies, lies, denials, and "I love only you and Raquel." I was thinking, what should I do? I couldn't continue this way. My family was living in Florida now, but even if they were in town, I wouldn't dare confide in them. I am a Serbian woman, and we are taught this is our shame. Now I know for sure this is not accurate thinking. I should have listened to the messenger on the telephone more intently. Shortly after the telephone call, and while I was trying to decide what to do, I noticed some alarming changes in my private parts. I went to see a doctor. The doctor informed me I had gonorrhea. I was paralyzed. Where does a husband go to get gonorrhea? Lord, where does anyone go to get that disease? I had never been compelled to cheat on my marriage, and besides, I had far too many problems to start new ones. I was confident I did not go anywhere or do anything to expose myself to this disease.

I was angry. I wish laws and consequences existed to punish the married cheater and the partner he/she cheats with because, in my observation and my personal experience, a cheater and his/her partner have no moral compass; they cause anguish to the spouse and the children in the family.

I came home from the doctor's office and worked on calming myself down. I paced lake a leopard. I had a conversation with myself—who else could I turn to with this horrible situation? What should I do about it? Where could I seek help?

I confronted Ed. Ed acted shocked as usual. He began his denials, lies, and more lies. He tried to question me how I might have gotten gonorrhea, and the more he went in that direction, the more incensed I became. I threw him out of the house. When I quieted down, I decided I must get a divorce before he brought worse diseases upon me and my child was left an orphan.

The next day, I went to an attorney to draw up divorce papers.

While I was waiting for my divorce papers, Ed terrorized me and Raquel. He would do things like wait until night fell and get a ladder and try to look through the windows into the bedrooms on the second floor of the house. I went to visit my parents' old friends, and he would follow me and run me off the road. He was scary, at the very least. I was becoming increasingly alarmed at his behavior. He vacillated between begging to reconcile and scaring me to death. He accused me of cheating. *Horrible!*

Finally, I thought I was going to be free. My divorce papers were ready. I called him to set up a meeting for him to sign the divorce papers. He wouldn't sign. He pleaded everything would be better, that he would try harder. Still the same old promises seven years later. He realized I was serious, and he called my mother and cried to her that he made a mistake, that he loved his family, that he'd do anything.

I Sought Help, I Got an Attorney, I Prepared Divorce Papers, So Why Didn't I Get Divorced?

Lord, you would think at this juncture my mother and I would have learned some lessons. The words Ed used every time he created a crisis for the past seven years were the same in nature, as my mother told me on several occasions, with the words my father used when he was begging her not to divorce him. But no, apparently, neither of us learned anything. She heard him out, called me, and conveyed a motherly message as she saw it. "Dragana, you have a child now. Do you want to repeat my mistake and get a divorce? Do you want Raquel to have a step-father like you did?" Well, now that she put it that way, I was paralyzed. Naive is as naive does. It did not dawn on me that I did not have to remarry and have a stepfather for Raquel, but the fear of following in her footsteps on that account scared me enormously. All fear, no logic!.

My mother's rationale was just an added weight as I was sinking. I had many more reasons that I was sinking, and hers just pulled me under faster. It had been seven years since I made the error of marrying Ed. During the seven years, he did what he wanted to do, and I focused and hid behind my job and Raquel. Every time I received a call from some female to tell me about Ed and their association and I confronted him, he would rant and yell and call me a stupid fucking bitch, always making shit up. When I brought up his brawling or whatever reason we had to bail him out of jail, he would tell me it was none of my fucking business. Sorry about the vulgarity, but it is what it is. He felt emboldened by my not acting on my divorce. I could see this was his way and nothing would change. I finally understood what my mother meant when, years ago, she told me I had made my bed and now I must lie in it. It meant I would have to put up with abuse and neglect while I continued working and taking care of my child and the bills while he did whatever immoral, sociopathic type of personalities did. The next time I brought up leaving or divorce, he stepped up his control game. Before I had Raquel, his control was berating and belittling me at home and in front of people, and once I had Raquel, he stepped up his threats of physical harm, like "Try leaving, I can get a drug addict to knock you off for $200." We lived in Chicago, where I saw violence every day, and I began to believe him. My fear for my life superseded my fear of leaving Raquel behind as an orphan with this insanity. This fear set up worked for him until five years after my final divorce in 1993.

When he thought I was no longer afraid of him or that I was becoming too secure in my profession and income, he stepped up his game once again. After I had two children, his new threat was, he would take the girls to Texas and tell them I was dead, that I would never find them and they would never look for me. I continued to believe his threats. In those days, kids were not as astute as they are now. There were no cell phones for me to teach them how to find me. Horrible, helpless feeling, especially if you do not confide in friends who can tell you otherwise.

Hindsight

Well, in hindsight, I realize I made a grave error not telling my attorney and my mother that although Ed did not get some bar singer pregnant like Peter did, he did the next best thing. He gave me a grievous social disease. I knew for sure, if I was open with my attorney and Vera, they would have given me different advice.

Ed returned home. Raquel and I were apprehensive. She was five years old. She was old enough to know what her father did was scary. Once in the home, Ed acted crazy. He was convinced I was having an affair, and he had someone follow me. He was back in the house for a few months, and I got pregnant with my second daughter, Erin. So unexpected! Talk about life unfolding at its own pace. Finally, our second daughter, Erin, was born, and the months of gestation lined up with the months necessary in Ed's mind. I said, "Lord, does this ever end?"

The day I came home with the baby, we moved to Tecumseh, Michigan, smack in the middle of cornfields. Good, I thought, this move would minimize Ed's temptations.

I often pondered if I should have let my mother be my life's architect, because I certainly did not build a good life for myself. At this point in time, I did not recognize that her experiences made her my yesterday's woman. Ed and I had nothing in common. I had ethics, he had none; I had morals, he had none. I believed in God, and he did not. I believed in a family home environment and spouse loyalty, and he had no such understanding or desire. I believed in a work ethic, and he had no such belief. At times I wondered if maybe there was something to matchmaking.

Hindsight

It is my firm belief from experience that matching morals, spiritual beliefs, loyalty, and ethics when choosing a mate promote a peaceful home life, and to do otherwise results in living a life in constant turmoil and despair.

CHAPTER SIX

TECUMSEH, MICHIGAN–
A FRESH START 1973

**Is It Possible to Have a Wonderful Dream
While Your House Is on Fire?
Yes, Until You Feel the Heat**

I would like to insert one very important and tragic point here as it relates to Ed. When it suited him, he could charm the pants off anyone, man, woman, or child. He can make people from all walks of life like him and children follow him. Everyone I know of who knew Ed in his business or personal life thought Ed was likeable and intelligent. If you were to ask any of his coaches (he played baseball, football, track, hockey), they would tell you he was a smart and skilled athlete. They would also tell you that this was true until something in his brain clicked and he spoiled the good work he did.

Shortly after his college graduation, one of Ed's coaches, who had known Ed for years and who had experienced how smart and skilled Ed could be, recommended him for a coaching job in Tecumseh, Michigan. We talked it over, I agreed to go, and he decided to take the job. Ed left for Tecumseh to find a place for us to live and to report to the high school where he was to assume his position. Meanwhile, I placed our house for sale and awaited Erin's birth. A few weeks after Ed started his new job, I gave birth to Erin. She, too, was a sweet and beautiful baby, like her sister, Raquel. She was not a crier. She brought love to both me and Raquel, and she still does. She was so tiny, with a full head of jet-black hair, and I was madly in love with her. I came home two days after I gave birth. Ed had the moving van packed with our belongings, and upon my arrival from the hospital, we left for Tecumseh.

Ed picked out a beautiful home on a cul-de-sac near a school for Raquel. Our backyard was a cornfield. Winter was beautiful there. We experienced snowdrifts for the first time. In summer, I had a little garden in the backyard, with carrots, tomatoes, and such. I sewed clothes for Raquel and Erin. I thought that year or so in Tecumseh was our best time as a couple and as a family. The children were healthy. I didn't go back to work that year. On Sundays, Ed and I would play cards and watch TV, and we would play with the children for hours. It was obvious he adored the girls, and the girls adored him. After all the turmoil, I genuinely tried to forgive and forget. I allowed myself to like this Ed I was living with. Once again, hope soared. Ed coached the high school cross-country team. He would have the boys run from the high school to our house, say hello, and return to school. I never thought anything of that. In fact, as we got to know the boys, it was kind of fun to see them. It never occurred to me that I was overseeing the track team. If I thought of it that way I might have wondered where was the coach?

I became a Blue Birds leader. The Blue Birds was a girls' club, like the Girl Scouts; only the Blue Birds was for the seven-year-old age group. It was fun teaching the girls how to do projects. I even recruited the music teacher at Raquel's school to teach the girls caroling for the holidays. I took the girls to the local establishments to sing, and everyone loved it. It was all so joyful.

I made a couple of friends in the neighborhood, and those friendships minimized the isolation in the boonies where we lived.

I planned to return to my position with American Airlines in the Detroit office the following year, but American Airlines had decided to move the Chicago and Michigan offices to Texas. I postponed my decision about work for the following year.

One Minute, I Was Living the Dream, the Next Minute, My Dream Was on Fire

How could it be that I was living a picture-perfect life one minute, and the next minute, with no warning, I was innocently answering the telephone and the speaker on the other end was yelling obscenities at me for what my husband was doing outside of the home? My husband remained calm, as though nothing was happening. He told me he just pissed off some people. *No big thing.* I knew Ed could piss people off, so I believed he just pissed people off. That, in comparison with what was coming, was acceptable. Of course I believed it. That is what all abused and controlled women have in common—we eventually take the path of least resistance, and we begin to accept the controller's lies, the idea being that believing their lies keeps peace. And lied he did. The next day, the calls continued, this time threatening, "If you value your family, you better leave town immediately." I asked the callers what was happening, but they wouldn't say. I leaped from being alarmed to being afraid. That leap was accurate, because the next day, the police called, asking for Ed. I was told we must leave town in two weeks. Ed had us moved within days. How could it be that we were ordered to leave our home? How could it be that Ed lost his teaching job and his certification when everything appeared to be going so well? To this day, I do not know what happened. This chaos came upon me so suddenly, and years later, I am still shocked by the entire event. This was to be one of many jobs he lost due to his unacceptable actions in the workplace.

This was my life with Ed. Right then, I realized there was no way to look forward to a peaceful life. After this event, even when it was peaceful, I was always waiting for the other shoe to drop, and Ed never disappointed me. He created chaos for me and himself all the years we were married. After this event, my heart was never fully open to loving or being loved by a man.

We had to make an immediate decision if we should return to Chicago or move to Texas or Florida. I wanted to move to Dallas, Texas, because I could resume my career with American Airlines. I was with American for seven years, had a few promotions, and I knew my work was respected there. Ed was adamant he did not want to move to Texas, so we decided to move to St. Petersburg, Florida. By this time, my parents lived in St. Petersburg. They owned two motels, so the rationale was, we could help them with the motel activity until we got situated.

The Drive from Tecumseh, Michigan, to St. Petersburg, Florida

It was good that the drive between Tecumseh and St. Petersburg was long, because it gave me time to think hard and make self-preservation decisions. I sat in the car and sorted things out fast and furious. I repeatedly asked myself hard and scary questions:

1. What is my situation now that I have two children?
2. What must I do to isolate myself and the children from Ed's constant jolts of insanity?
3. What are my options?

4. I have no job. How can I move forward with my personal growth and security?

And the most important question of all:

5. Once I find these answers, how can I implement my solutions without arousing his fears, which may bring down his wrath on all three of us? Most importantly, my plan must work within Ed's parameters. He must feel like he owns us, controls us in submission, and does not feel the threat of abandonment.

I thought only God could help me, because at that time I was making this plan, it all seemed impossible. I didn't dare believe in myself, so I used God as my surrogate. To me to believe in God was to believe in myself. At this point, I was thinking like I was a captured prisoner of war trying to escape.

I mentioned in previous chapters that I planned the first apartment move, I planned the finances to purchase our first home, and I planned how I could purchase our first home.

I am a planner, and I work my plan. I don't know how I would have achieved as much as I have without this mentality. So in a nutshell, I came up with a plan for my existence until Erin graduated from high school. She was two years old.

This plan was my guidebook.

I gave myself hope that I would be free when Erin graduated from high school. This timeline removed the threat that Ed could ever remove her from me. I would feel save then. She would be at college.

The basic conclusion about my situation was that I was going to need to have minimum expectations from Ed, like collecting his paycheck to pay the bills. This was not as easily done as said. I tried not to involve emotions such as caring, because caring meant we would have to meet some standard for marriage, like being on the same page about morality, unity, and consideration. After seven years' experience living with Ed, I knew for sure Ed did not have any of these qualities in him.

The way I looked at my options was, I could leave Ed, maybe my family would support me, and maybe not. If the family did support me, the prospect of returning to my family's lifestyle would be more devastating because my stepfather did not mellow. Once a wife-beater, always a wife-beater. It would be a tough world raising two pretty girls as a single mom and working. Mainly, I didn't want to put it past him that he would take the girls out of state and tell them I was dead, nor did I want to put it past him, particularly after this last scary event in Michigan, that he might have me murdered by some drug addict. There it was; I was a poster woman for what abused women's thinking looks like!

The answer to how I could move forward with my personal growth and security was complicated, because up until then, I was my mother's keeper, my half-sister and brother's keeper, and Ed's keeper. How could I figure out a way to measure my own needs and growth?

So here it is. This was what I came up with, and I encourage all women in healthy and unhealthy relationships to try it.

See yourself as a pie and divide the pie in three equal pieces. Label the pieces as such:

a) Me and my personal needs, growth, career, home
b) My relationships (mate, friends, extended family)
c) My children, grandchildren

Think of each piece as one-third then hold on tight to the numbers. The premise is, if you are giving in, giving up, or dedicating more than one-third of your day, your month, or your year to someone else, you are not saving time to dedicate to your personal needs, growth, and achievements.

I know this technique works. I know, too, to make it work, you must be your own advocate.

I worked hard to implement my solutions without arousing his fears, which may bring down his wrath on all three of us.

Hindsight

In hindsight, I must admit, although the plan gave me hope and cleared a path in my thinking, my plan was flawed. While I was trying to avoid Ed's wrath, I sacrificed much in my and my daughters' lives. I will never know if this sacrifice was less than what the results would have been if I divorced Ed when I got to St. Petersburg, Florida. The answer might depend on what degree of danger was perceived versus real. Either way, I was scared to gamble.

St. Petersburg, Florida

Upon our arrival in St. Petersburg, we stayed with my parents. They lived in a grand neighborhood, in a spacious house. The backyard was lovely and peaceful, with beautiful flowers, a picnic table down the middle of the yard draped with grapevines, and a large pool. Sadly, this was the only thing peaceful in my parents' home. In a matter of days, I said to myself out loud, while standing in the backyard, after a Roy-and-Vera yelling match, "How did I end up in the same house with Roy, Vera, and Ed?"

The children were little, especially Erin—she was two years old. My mother thought I should go all day to the motel with her and my sister Zorica to clean rooms and, in the evening, help her with rentals and bookkeeping and leave Ed with the children. That worked for a while, until Ed decided I needed to spend more time with the children so he could go out to look for a job. I was in the middle, but I agreed with Ed. He did need to get a job so we could get a home of our own. Eventually, I got my courage up to talk to my mother and explain the situation from our perspective. My mother was miffed, but we compromised; I would help her a few hours a day then take care of the children while Ed looked for a job. Within a year, we purchased a nice little house in a pleasant neighborhood and an apartment rental building. Ed tried to manage the rentals, but not for long. I maintained all the books and rented and cleaned the apartments out when they were vacant. He needed to get a job to bring in income. It wasn't long before Ed got a job with Wendy's as manager, a couple of blocks from my mother's motel. My parents knew the district manager because they often ate at that Wendy's, so they put in a good word for Ed. Since he was fifteen, when he came to our house with a summer jacket in the middle of a snowstorm, my mother had always had sympathetic feelings for Ed. That was because she didn't know him.

In a short period, we sold the apartment building and made a reasonable turnover profit. Once Ed started his job, and from the proceeds of our Michigan house, we purchased a bigger home not far from our first home in St. Petersburg. The new home was lovely, spacious, with an over-the-garage apartment just in case Ed's ailing mother needed to live with us. It was located near Raquel's school and a nice park, where the kids enjoyed playing.

On Sundays, everyone would gather at my mother's house, where we would eat, drink, and swim all day. Majority of the time, it was mostly enjoyable, unless Roy decided to needle my mother, at which point a fight would ensue and the day would go to pot.

I found a part-time job with AAA in their travel department. I liked the job. It was in my line of experience, and I was comfortable there. In a short period, AAA promoted me to take care of reservations, tour ticketing, and the office bookkeeping. I liked that job also. The deeper I got into the job, the more I realized I knew the mechanics, but I did not know the whole scope of general ledger bookkeeping. So I enrolled in a college bookkeeping class. All part of my plan for my personal growth and security. As I said before, it is crazy how a circumstance can take on a life of its own. Not long after I finished my bookkeeping class, AAA agreed with Agency Data Systems, a small computer company, to test the first interface between the airline reservations computers and the back-office bookkeeping computer. I was part of their success. Not long after the success of the software implementation, Agency Data Systems offered me a full-time position with their company. The offer came at a perfect time. Erin was old enough to be in day care, Raquel was in school, and I was ready to take on a full-time job. I accepted the offer and started working full-time in Tampa.

Once again, everything seemed to be on track. We had been in Florida for a couple of years then. We had healthy, good children. We had a beautiful home. We had good jobs and good income.

And Then *Boom*

One day, my sister and I were entering my house with the children. The telephone was ringing, and so I answered it. A woman on the other end of the telephone was screaming, "Your disgusting husband slept with my son's girlfriend in my son's bedroom! We caught him sneaking out of the house!"

I felt my blood drain to my feet. All I could say was, "Oh my god."

My sister caught on that something was wrong, so she asked, "What is happening?"

I didn't answer my sister. I exclaimed to the woman, "That can't be!" And I asked her, "How do you know it was my husband?"

She responded, screaming, "Because the young girl works for him at Wendy's!"

I repeated, "Oh my god, that can't be!"

The woman screamed, "Yes, it is true!"

This conversation is burned into my memory. I can recall it like it was yesterday. This was sheer insanity. It was bad enough he was cheating, but in someone else's home? It was so outrageous! No one can just make this stuff up!

I sat, waiting for Ed to come home, and I began to connect his taking my virginity by force, all the letters I found in the Bible from girls he was trying to convince to sleep with him, the unknown reason he lost his teaching job, and now this sixteen-year-old. I didn't know what to do with this information.

As I had done several times before, I confronted Ed when he came home from wherever he was. He swore he didn't know anything about what this woman was talking about. *Deny, deny, deny.* He offered an explanation that it might be someone he fired trying to get back at him. For the sake of my sanity, I wanted to believe his explanation, but the caller was an older woman, she sounded genuinely upset, and I knew better. When I persisted with the conversation, he went into his usual rants and name-calling when he got caught in his lies, always ending his rant with "You are a stupid, fucking-crazy bitch, always making shit up!" Without fail, that was his standard response to me as he stormed out of the house.

I tried to reason this out, but I didn't know what to do about this incident. I reminded myself of the five points in my plan I prepared while driving from Michigan. That calmed the pain in my heart. I reassured myself with the thought that for sure, I was leaving when Erin graduated from high school. I didn't tell myself her graduation was fifteen years away.

While Persevering

I reminded myself to tend to my mental health, my education, and my financial stability. These were the elements that would supply the power I needed to regain and maintain ownership of my own destiny.

The next day, I went about my business, and as usual, I took the children to school, I went to work, I picked up the children from school, etc. When I came home, Ed was not home. I thought he was at work—he often worked evenings. Shortly after I settled in, the telephone rang. I answered the telephone, and it was my mother on the other end.

"Hello, Dragana," she said.

You may recall, that is my Serbian name. Although I had changed it legally to Ann, my mother and all my Serbian friends called me Dragana.

I knew that tone. Something was up. Here it was: she called me to ask why Ed was no longer working at Wendy's. She stated that the people at the restaurant told her he was let go two weeks ago. I didn't know what to say to my mother. I didn't know how much she knew. I suspected she knew more than she was telling. I didn't want to rile myself up again. I told her I didn't know the reason, that she could ask him herself when she saw him on Sunday. We hung up the telephone. Ed was coming and going every day as though he was going to work.

I was doing it again. I didn't tell my mother what was happening. I had my reasons clearly stated in my escape plan. I didn't pursue this matter much further for fear that the surging insanity might force me to take some rash action. I moved forward, and I focused on the two-thirds of my life that was sane, my work and children.

It turned out Ed was let go from his job over a week before my mother told me he no longer had a job. Fortunately, Ed was already looking for a job. It wasn't long before he got a job with Pizza Hut in Tampa.

Neither of us pursued the telephone call I received or the loss of his job. I knew there would be no point in arguing because lies would only inflame the situation, and I had my exit plan.

By 1982, we were both employed in the Tampa area. I was employed by American Airlines, and Ed was employed by PepsiCo's Pizza Hut. Our home and children's schools were still in St. Petersburg. St. Petersburg and Tampa are connected by a bridge. Before the bridge was rebuilt, the old bridge used to flood. Shortly after both of us were working in Tampa, a storm flooded the bridge. We could not cross the bridge until the water subsided. Fortunately, my mother and sister took care to pick up the children from school. This challenge facilitated our decision to sell our house in St. Petersburg and move to Tampa.

CHAPTER SEVEN

TAMPA, 1982–1993

Tampa, Winding Road to Freedom

At this juncture of my storytelling, I had to take a pause in my writing. Old memories and fears flooded my mind. Ed's old threats began to infect my mind with fear. I began to worry about Ed's reaction to my writing this book. I stopped writing for a few weeks, taking time out to determine if my fears of Ed's old threats were greater than my courage. It was apparent he had moved on with his life. The question now was, have I? Before I could continue writing, I had to answer, am I still in his clutches somehow? And there it was, the same conclusion I made when I decided to make Ed move out for the final time. The answer was, I would rather die than be in his clutches and fear him again. Armed with my answer and some encouragement from dear friends, I refocused, and here I am to continue my story.

I am constantly saved by the self-preservation plan I created during my trip from Tecumseh to St. Petersburg. Dividing my life in three parts, personal growth, relationships, and children, saved me because when my relationship with Ed became unbearably painful, I could visualize that only one-third of my life was in disarray, and the other two-thirds was satisfying and joyful. My work was satisfying, and my children brought me joy. I invite the reader to keep my rationale in mind as you read about my trials and tribulations because if you, or someone you know, are in a similar situation, applying my plan may help minimize hopelessness while you are working your way out of your situation.

It was 1982, ten long years to go before I could claim my individual existence. Many changes occurred in this ten-year life span. Often, I asked myself, could I endure the next ten years? At times, I was, and still am, deeply saddened that I wished the best years of my life away. Here it is that hindsight, again, If I had to do it all over again, I would disregard my mother's and Ed's aggression and control and move into that first one-bedroom apartment alone and start my life on my own terms. I would repeat this regret in this writing as I have in my mind many, many times. So if you are in a similar situation, I hope you will consider my conclusions. No one ever realized or appreciated my sacrifices, not my mother, not my husband, not my children. At times, they were unforgiving of my unhappiness; often, they voiced that they thought I was not moving on fast enough. How could they understand sacrificing so much for so long? After my divorce, everyone moved on. I was stuck in the rubble of my shattered life and soul that I was left with. It took another ten years before I felt strong enough to walk into my new life. It is hard, at times impossible, to move on when everything about your life is either painful to look back on or simply not there. Hindsight is wonderful if you wish to recount your regrets. Seeking council from yesterday's women, like your mother, grandmother, elderly neighbor, or a stranger who has lived a full life, is priceless. Their advice can help you minimize regrets. For me, it was too late. I didn't have the courage to seek advice, so I let life unfold like an airplane with an insane pilot.

Here we were at another start—new town, new jobs, new homes. I knew better, but I once again hoped and prayed we could just have a peaceful home environment. I purchased a piano for the girls to enjoy taking piano lessons. We enrolled the girls in a nice small private school to ensure they would get a good education. They were lovely, agreeable children, and I felt joy when I was with them. I loved my job. It was most satisfying. My clients were successful businesspeople. So two-thirds of my life was satisfying. As for my relationship with Ed, at this point, I built a tall wall around my emotions to isolate myself from his abuse and neglect. I realized, the higher the wall, the less daylight I got, so even that was a no-win situation.

Frankly, I don't know how Raquel and Erin survived the tension in the household, but God is good, and they turned out to be wonderful women. The girls were my pride and joy, and they still are. Their sweetness softened the brutality that life sometimes bestowed upon me. They are in their forties now, and they are wives and mothers. They are loving and caring wives and mothers, but their struggles are apparent; they are lacking good role models that Ed and I should have provided during their teenage years. Instead, Ed bit down on our lives like a dog bites into a raggedy doll.

The next ten years were really and truly filled with Ed commandeering our lives with meanness and fury. Everything was pretty much on his timetable and his demands. Let me give a brief recap of events to lend some insight into what this means.

One day, Raquel and Erin went to a roller-skating rink. Raquel was about twelve, and Erin was seven years old. They had a good time with their friends, and while they were there, a roller-skating coach noticed them and invited them to join his roller-skating team. The girls were excited about the idea.

At that time, it all seemed like it would be fun for the girls and would give them something to do. This was the furthest idea possible from what happened. This sport took on a life of its own and took the children with it. I cannot express the despair I felt, and at times still feel, that I gave in to allowing the girls to join a roller-skating team. The sport was brutal. The training was brutal. And Ed was brutal.

Once on the team, the girls started making great strides, especially Raquel, because she was older. It was apparent to everyone that she was a fine athlete—great speed and hand-and-eye coordination. Not to slight Erin, but she was only seven years old; the competition was not as intense at that age as it was with the teenagers. The recruiting coach was kind to the girls. He was his daughter's brutal coach, so he learned from that experience. Raquel made great progress rapidly, and her natural talent became apparent to the coach and Ed. Ed decided to take over Raquel's coaching. He formed a team of his own for that purpose. I am firmly convinced after observing my husband coaching his children, my sons-in-law coaching their children, and other fathers alike that fathers should feed their egos some other way. Instead of pounding their children, they should be their children's greatest fans. Somehow, this man could be good to everyone except his family, especially Raquel. He was brutal. He forced her to train day and night literally, and with the senior boys. There was very little time to do family or fun mother-daughter things. In those years, the best I could do was tag after the girls to make sure they were safe. He would pick up the children from school, they would change their clothes, and they would eat in the car on their way to practice. By the time they came home, they were exhausted. After a while, Ed began to run additional practices in the middle of the night for the older children. He would rouse Raquel from her sleep to take her to train in a cold, dumpy roller rink. At the same time, she had to get up in the early morning to go to school.

If this was not challenging enough, he was verbally abusive to her in front of her peers and other adults.

For example, one year, during a national competition, he yelled at her with filthy language in front of hundreds of people. I was sick; I couldn't stand for him to be in the same room with Raquel. He slept outside of our hotel room that night. Some competitors gave Raquel a hard time, and they resented her. The people around us felt great compassion for her because of his treatment. She was the only girl who had to ride her bike to the competition, while others drove and rested. He was relentless, but the poor girl never complained. At times, she just cried quietly.

The only way I could stay connected with the girls was to trail after them. He would have the children ride up to one hundred miles on open roads, where there were no designated bike lanes. Out of fear for the children at times, I would follow behind them with my car half on the road, half on the roadside shoulder. Impatient, people would yell and throw things at the children. I was frantic with worry every time they went on those rides. Eventually, this training took a toll on Raquel's school grades. I feared she would fall too far behind and not be able to graduate. But what could I do? She was an excellent athlete, and everyone thought she could be the national champion. She worked too hard, and she was eventually invited to train in the Olympic Training Center. I couldn't pull her out until the championship meets were over.

There was no talking to Ed—his importance came first. In his mind, he was a great coach. I compromised with my fears, and I decided to wait until the minute Raquel collected her awards for her hard work and sacrifices then pulled her out of the sport. The sport was going nowhere. It was not like it was going to the Olympics or she could gain a scholarship out of it; the only thing that could happen was, she could fail to graduate with her class. I was thankful that in junior year of high school, she won the national championship. Once she collected her award, I took her out of the sport and freed her to enjoy her senior year of high school. I am grateful she had the strength and wisdom to agree with that decision.

Of course, it was always all about Ed. He lost his champion and the attention he got from training her. The minute I took Raquel out of the sport, Ed lived in the same house but refused to speak to Raquel for two months. It was painful for her, especially since he diverted his attention toward her sister, Erin. Once this transpired, I was split between Erin's and Raquel's needs. Erin was on the training circuit, and Raquel was home. Often, Erin would call me in panic because Ed would give no credence to the fact that she was a young girl. To help other athletes, he would let them, mostly boys, pile into his and Erin's hotel room. More than once, I had to get a second room for her when she would call in a panic. It always perplexed me why he never tended to his family's needs first. My conclusion to this question was that he needed attention, so when he did things for others, that was what he got, attention. So he took his children for granted.

I tried to keep up with Erin to make sure she was doing well. She progressed nicely, ultimately won the regional championships, and was smart enough to get out of the sport on her own to prepare for high school. At an early age, Erin was an independent spirit. For example, her freshman year, she decided she did not want to go to private high school like her sister, so one day, before school year started, she sat me down to tell me that with the help of her friend's mother, she had enrolled herself in a public school she preferred to attend. She asked me if

I would sign the permission papers. I approved of her decision; after all, it was an excellent school. I admired her independence.

Between my job and his job and coaching roller-skating, Ed and I were like two ships crossing the sea. We rarely sat down to talk like spouses or friends. On holidays, he would barely participate, often coming in late for special events like birthdays, Christmas dinners, graduations. We were always like an afterthought or an inconvenience for him. This was clear to all three of us. During this ten-year period, we did not take family vacations. However, it was later disclosed Ed did take vacations to various golfing resorts with various friends. Mercy. As close as I came to a vacation was one year, I was a designated driver to take four teenagers to Couderay, Wisconsin. A scary, long, and fun drive. Oh my goodness! The children could be fun! We stayed in a rented house near an Indian reservation. While the children were training every day, I would walk to the small store down the road from where we were staying and pick up a beer and a lotto scratch-off ticket. I would sit on the boat dock overlooking a peaceful lake, surrounded by beautiful trees and birds chirping, drink a beer, and scratch off my ticket to see if I was a winner. During a week's time, I won twice—first time I won $10, and the second time, I won $50. With my winnings, for the fun of it, I would buy a bunch of cake and ice cream for the children. We all had a wonderful time.

While at the training camp, my Raquel bonded with a young skater. Steve was his name. He was from somewhere in California. When Raquel graduated from high school, she informed us she intended to move to California to live with Steve. I almost lost my mind. She was eighteen years old and had never lived away from home before. California was so far from Florida. But like with Erin, what could I do? I could not say no. She was determined to go. I knew Raquel and I had a strong bond, which gave me confidence that she knew if she needed me, I would be there for her promptly. So her father and I stood in the driveway, crying like a pair of saps as our eighteen-year-old daughter pulled away in her little BMW loaded up with her belongings, with her boyfriend in the passenger seat. All I could do at this juncture was pray for her safety, and I did just that. I traveled often to visit with Raquel. She was, and still is, a clever and responsible girl. She found a nice place to live, had a part-time job, and enrolled in the local college.

Four Years To Go

Erin started high school and played softball. She was a fine athlete and a good student. I was always very proud of her. In many ways, her sense of independence gave me strength to move forward with my plan to free myself. Erin's start in high school signified that I only had four years to go before I would leave this marriage. The week Erin started high school, I recall feeling defiant, hopeful, and skeptical all at the same time. Suddenly, it was like seeing a light at the end of the tunnel—it was all near, within reach, a completely different feeling than twenty years or ten years before. The end of the tunnel near, I could see the sun.

Note to the Reader

If you are in a healthy relationship and believe a friend is not, give her as much love and support as you can to help her free herself.

If you are a person in a relationship that resembles mine, please seek out friends who are strong and loyal and have the courage to tell them your story and count on them to help you free yourself. Life is very short, and you cannot get back the years and opportunities you miss. Don't waste them.

A Case for Believing in Destiny?

Long ago, an old Serbian woman said to me, "No matter how many detours you take, destiny will find you."

While Raquel was in California, an incredible event occurred. One day out of the blue, as the saying goes, a young girl called, saying her name was Helena, that she was the daughter of my sister Maria, and asked me if I happened to be her aunt Dragana. I get the chills just writing this sentence. I was so thrilled I was crying. The feeling of finally having some connection to my brother and sisters was pure elation. Helena stated she and her sister Vesna were in California, working as nannies. I could not believe my good fortune. I flew to California immediately. It was a joyful event. Finally, after searching for and longing to find them for almost thirty years, I was connected to all my beloved siblings and my sweet aunt. Shortly after I met the girls in California, I went to Serbia, where we gathered for the first time after thirty years. Before I met my family in Serbia, I knew I was grossly unhappy. When I saw their warm smiles and tears as they greeted me, I realized how lonely, deflated, and empty my soul was from living with Ed without love and caring. The minute this realization came over me, I knew for sure, no matter what, I was to free myself of Ed's tyranny. This was the most healing event of my life. In the very short time that I was around my family, the child in me was revived. I was flooded with the goodness I knew before I left Serbia.

It is worth describing my first meeting with my siblings in Serbia because it demonstrates how strong childhood bonds are. Children form everlasting bonds with love for one another, with great innocence and purity that nothing can break. When we first met, we were all in our late forties, yet we hugged and cried as we did so long ago when we were young children between the ages of ten and thirteen. It was somewhat surprising that they, too, felt abandoned by my departure, even though they knew

I had no choice but to leave. They said my departure created a gaping hole in their play and everyday activities. We started our conversations as though we were the age I left, ranging from ten to thirteen. We talked and teased using the same childish teasing statements. We recalled the same funny things we did, the athletic competitions, the things that caused a spanking or a teacher's punishment. They were used to me sitting on their laps. As they alternated hugging me, they would pull me on their lap or next to them on their chairs. I could feel the healing. I could feel the loneliness diminishing and the special feelings I had before I left Serbia returning. I swelled like a peacock filled with tremendous emotions. I was connected once again to the life that was full of love and care. It felt like I found a bridge over all the years of neglect and void of love and affection. This meeting with my siblings was life-altering, and it breathed life into me.

When I wrote about my mother's circumstances, I wrote briefly about the hardships for the citizens of Serbia under the dictator Tito. I noted that only the top layers of the Communist Party had jobs, food, shelter, and medicine, which prompted many to defect to other countries. This was true for my mother's generation and my brother and sisters' generation as well. My brother, Dusan, lived in France, sister Maria lived in Sweden, and Bisa lived in Germany. Nowadays, we meet up every few years either in Paris or Serbia. It is never easy to leave one's birth country, because you must leave behind familiar traditions, mores, and the love of family. As immigrants, my siblings have their own challenging stories to tell.

The stories I am sharing are truthful. I know people with normal households can't imagine why a person will stay in such a destructive relationship, but the women who are in similar relationships know what I am writing is sad and truthful.

The Last Year

Urgency, for courage and dignity, flooded my senses.

The ending was on the horizon. If I could see the light at the end of the tunnel when Erin started high school, now in her senior year, I was in the sunlight and the tunnel was behind me.

In my mind, I was packed and ready to go.

About a year or so before I would seek my freedom, Ed's tyranny and insanity exceeded creepy. I was living it but could not believe it. Truly, I was often in disbelief of what I was hearing and experiencing. At times, I questioned my senses. Thank goodness my friends and children saw it also.

We were barely ever intimate. Usually, when he did something bad, he did the begging and the pleading and acted extra-attentive and considerate, like he was changed. I think nowadays, people call it makeup sex. In retrospect, I don't know what one would call it when you are intimate under the tyranny and fear of reprisal while the lunatic is insisting he is changed, and because he says so, you must act like you believe it.

A few weeks or so after I was intimate with Ed, I began to itch in my private parts. As a practice, I believe personal hygiene to be very important daily. I am very clean about myself, so I couldn't understand what could be the problem. I knew Ed was itching for several weeks before me. When I asked him about it, he told me he had jock itch. That made sense to me because he was athletic. He ran every day, and so on. He stated he was using some sort of powder for that condition. Now I was itching as well. Since I did not practice any sports activity, I was perplexed. I changed soaps, took extra showers, yet for the next few days, the itching did not subside. I took a close look with a magnifying glass, and oh my god, it looked like I had some sort of bug attached to my skin! I was frantic, frantic, frantic. I pulled one out and put it under the magnifying glass. I swear I was hysterical. Whom could I turn to for advice? I had the same horrified feeling as when I found out Ed gave me gonorrhea. I immediately turned to my gynecologist. Oh, oh, oh, I was in disbelief when he told me I had the crabs. I never even heard of such things. I swear these things truly do look like a miniature crab. Oh, thank goodness, to cure this horrible condition, all I had to do was purchase some type of liquid and wash with it. In a couple of days, I was free of the itching.

While I was purchasing the liquid for myself, I purchased a bottle for Ed. I went to his office, shut the door, and let him have it. I swear to you, his response and facial expressions were like he didn't know how I caught such a condition. As usual, with a straight face, he lied and denied he had the crabs, that only I did. Oh, and by the way, he did keep the liquid potion.

Once again, in agony, I ask, how does a married man get crabs? How does any man get them? Alas, as the exclamation goes, where do they go to get them? Finally, after the shock wore off, I decided that was the last time he would go near me—God knows where he went and what he did there. I didn't dare speculate because I feared what I might do. I must remain calm because Erin was in her last year of school. I must not disrupt her graduation!

Once again, I felt shame. I didn't tell anyone about this until after I was ready to get a divorce. By now I knew, if I told my mother, she would have backed me to get a divorce immediately. But I had Erin to consider, and by now, I only trusted myself and my plan.

It was at this juncture that I feared being with Ed ever again. This was such a jolt of reality that I realized if I could get these types of diseases, he could transmit something worse that could bring about my death, and my children would be devastated. As I am writing this story, I am still in shock over this incident, for some reason more so than I was over him giving me gonorrhea.

Hindsight

When people cheat on each other, friends and relatives see only the hurt; most everyone fails to imagine that the cheater can devastate lives with disease because of promiscuous behavior. I never thought of it this way either until this second incident. The first should have been more than enough for me to see the light, but naïveté is like blindness.

Like leopards, liars never change their spots.

Cheaters never change. It is like they have some sort of emotional disease, like a horrible addiction. I am an educated woman, I have a college degree in human development studies, and I did everything possible to give him support. I waited for twenty-seven years for his promises that he would change to come to fruition. He never changed; he just lied and pleaded better, and when that did not work, he resorted to stronger threats.

At this point, Ed and I had nothing in common. He was barely home. As I stated before, he would leave the house, and if anyone had to find him for any reason, no one knew where he was. In later years, he had a cell phone, yet we still could not reach him. He always had one reason or another why he did not answer. I had to travel for my business, and while out of town, I would call home to find the girls were alone, and they did not know where their father was or when he would be home. Thank goodness the girls were grown by then.

The only time it was apparent we were still married was when I would go out to dinner with colleagues. He would show up in restaurants to check whom I was with. His behavior was so embarrassing it put me on edge every time I had to meet people for dinner. That is what controllers do: they put people on edge. At times, he would do ridiculous and embarrassing things to keep me on edge. For example, one evening, I was with several people, some peers and some out-of-town clients, when one of the peers who knew Ed pointed at a man in the bushes and said, "Ann, I think your husband is spying on you. He is in the bushes." When I saw him, I was humiliated. To Ed, when he lied, his lies must become immediate truth to the listeners. He said he was just looking for me. Oh, in the bushes? His lies always made sense to him.

Believe it or not, after this incident, Ed went home. I called home, and my daughter Raquel told me not to come home. He was home crying, saying that he was sorry. His behavior became increasingly creepy.

Another example, American Airlines gave a Christmas party for the employees. He peered through the windows of the establishment, looking at all of us until one of my *married* peers asked me to dance. Guess what the control freak did? He came through the door and toward me like an angry bull. While everyone was looking on in disbelief, he grabbed me by the arm and pulled me out of the building. Everyone, except me, was shocked. I was simply humiliated. After many such events, I stopped accepting invitations for dinner, parties, or company outings with my peers. When I did attend out-of-town seminars or dinners with clients, I was constantly on edge, looking for him.

I was fortunate that I traveled for my business. My clients were gracious hosts. While out of town, I experienced the best possible social gatherings, beautiful places, resorts, restaurants, and events. As a regional manager of Latin and Central America for American Airlines, I experienced different cultures and social mores. I was pleased that I created my plan and taught myself to separate these rewarding events from my unpleasant and socially barren home environment. This was the one-third that was good.

Meanwhile, the control freak did whatever he wanted. I could go on and on about control freaks' intimidating actions, but it would serve no purpose for me or the reader, so I will continue with the events during the last year before my sweet Erin graduated—my breakout timeline.

I Held on to the Calendar for Dear Life, Counting Months

Generally, I was not invited to Ed's company events, particularly the last years of our marriage, with a few exceptions when wives were necessary for appearance's sake. When I did attend a function, Ed dumped me off with his assistant and acted like I was the enemy. That makes sense if you want the girlfriend to think what she needs to think to partner up in the cheater game. By then, between my cheater bosses in my various job positions and Ed, I had become an expert in spotting a cheater and his/her partner a mile away. Just for fun, here's an example.

It is a flag when the girlfriend's and/or employee's children are very, very, very familiar with your husband when in real life the child should barely know him. For example, one Halloween, Ed's assistant gave a party and invited all the families, Ed's and his supervisors'. One of the woman supervisor's child talked to Ed more intimately that his children would, teasing about who beat whom at basketball and stuff like that. Just a note, that meant Mr. Ed went to the supervisor's house frequently.

When I first noticed the obvious intimacy between Ed and the supervisor in question, I confronted him. Before I confronted Ed, I said to myself, *Thank God I have only seven months to go.* I can say, Ed's responses had not changed in twenty-six years. He acted out as usual. He lied, denied, and applied his verbal attacks as he always did when caught in a lie. Let me describe what this man looked like when he was caught in his web of lies. As he ranted, his face would form a snarl and his eyes would sharpen like a rattlesnake's. He would pick up his pace as he approached me and stop within inches of my face. When I was younger, I used to shut up and stand still, but this last year, I would just walk away, knowing I had to cure myself of fearing him, especially if I was to leave soon. While all this was happening, I was privately hoping this was a serious affair between him and this supervisor. I felt it would help free me if he had someone else he could control and use for stability. At this juncture, I knew I must prove to myself, once and for all, that they were a couple, because if they were a couple, my exit would be easier to accomplish. If they were not a couple, I was in for more of Ed's desperate, holding-on tactics, like pleading or threatening. On a more personal level, even though people call and tell you that your husband is a cheater, even though he gives you a social disease, the control freak's browbeating and intimidations are so convincing that it makes you doubt your own logic and reality—the denials and bullying blur your vision and self-confidence to the point that his lies and attacks become stronger than your senses. Perhaps this is the greatest phenomena that keeps women captive in abusive and punishing relationships.

In my mind, this was to be the last confrontation where he'd get to rant about me "making shit up," as he would put it. I was now determined to overcome my fears of Ed's threats of reprisal. Soon, Erin would be graduating and going away to college. At this point, I made up my mind I would rather die than continue to live in this nightmare with Ed. I set out to let myself off this self-doubt hook. The next event I had to face was Ed's district meeting in Atlanta, Georgia. I'd been in the corporate world for many years, and I knew this was not rare. What would be rare was if a supervisor was to attend a director's meeting. On that premise, I checked around to see if Ed's new best friend (we will call her Bertha, and after my divorce, we will call her Bertha) was staying in town. No, she was not. Now, I was working for Delta Airlines, and my base was Atlanta. I took a page out of Ed's playbook and took a seven o'clock flight to Atlanta and went directly to Ed's hotel. He was not there. I called all the surrounding hotels and found Bertha's hotel This was in the days when hotels still gave out guest's names. I showed up at the Holiday Inn, where she was staying, and saw Ed was there. I returned to the airport and took the next flight back to Tampa.

I was so rattled that it was noticeable to an elderly woman sitting next to me on the airplane. She spoke softly and said to me, "Dear, I don't know what is the matter, but if it's about a man, rid yourself of him as soon as you can." I swear this yesterday's woman was a stranger who gave me the best advice; more importantly, she gave me a great sense of empowerment. Her words echoed in my soul every time I panicked about leaving. I thought, *God speaks to us through others.*

When he came home, I purposely confronted Ed. The drill was the same as I described several times. I didn't care at this point, and I was glad it was true; I was just making a point for my sake more than anyone else's. At this point, I was out to solidify my own sanity and courage.

Next event I choose to address came at Christmastime. On Christmas Day, Ed received a telephone call. After he hung up, he said he must go to work. *Not really,* I said to myself. I decided to follow him. I did not realize my daughter Raquel had her own suspicions until we both ended up in the same place. There he was at a golf course, not at work, and there she was at the same golf course, waiting for him. She panicked when she saw me and Raquel and ran for the women's bathroom. I followed her just to see her cheater face, and I left. I didn't make a scene, okay, I made a little scene with Ed and left. That night, Ed came home and calmly conveyed a message to me, his wife, from a guy named Jay, who was Bertha's friend. The message was simple. It went something like this, "Jay stated he has many guns. If you go near this woman's house again, he is going to shoot you." Please, as you are reading this, can you even make this insane stuff up? Well, I was not to be deterred from my goal to solidify my sanity and courage. Now the game was on. I was in my pajamas when I received this message. It was almost store closing time, but I was not to be deterred!. I immediately changed my clothes, got into my car, and drove to Sports Unlimited, a sports equipment store. There, I purchased a nice .38-caliber gun. I didn't go home with my new gun because I tried to use good judgment. However, I did bring a pink copy of the proof of purchase receipt and handed it over to Ed. I said to him, "No one will ever get to hold me hostage or scare me again." Really! That was what I said. He had nothing to say, but I believe, from his befuddled facial expression, he was thinking maybe I meant it! I didn't bring my gun home until I had proper training at the local gun range. An equalizer is what I call it.

By the way, I don't advise anyone to purchase a gun to settle any arguments. I felt this was my last resort to convey to the abuser that I would not put up with any more abuse and control from anyone, him or his friends. I wanted him to know that I could act crazier than him, and at this point, I was beginning to believe I was! I did not tell anyone else about this purchase until after my divorce.

Later, I found out why Ed repeated Jay's threat. Apparently, after we left the golf course, where we had our emotional collision with Ed the liar and Bertha the cheater partner, my daughter Raquel somehow got a hold of a picture of Ed with his girlfriend, burned a hole in their faces, and hung the picture on her doorknob. They assumed the scorned wife did that deed. Just as a note, I would never expose myself by placing myself on their property. I follow this rule because I believe the cheater's girlfriends are as ruthless as the cheaters. Neither possess a moral compass.

While I was dealing with emotional strengthening, I was also preparing financially. When you have a small business, the income is feast-or-famine—meaning, the high months you make a wonderful income, and low-peak months' income is slow in coming in. I knew what was ahead, so I closed my business and accepted a more stable position with Delta Airlines. With Delta, I had insurance benefits and a steady income. I thought, between our savings and my income, I would have a reasonable new start. The best I can describe this understanding on my part is that I was dumb and happy. What savings?

It Was June 1992, and Erin Graduates from High School

I was very happy for many reasons. I think when a child graduates from high school, the event brings about many great feelings of joy and pride. She was a good student and a bright child. She is a teacher now, and I have great pride in her and her work.

First Day of Erin's Future and Mine

I came home from Erin's graduation with the resolve of a lion tamer. I informed Ed, that he had six hours to move anything he wanted in the house and then he was to leave and never return to the house until I was moved out. I stressed that if he did not comply, I would use a more aggressive approach. The next day, Ed moved the furniture he wanted into his new apartment.

His things were gone. God is good!

CHAPTER EIGHT

FLYING LESSONS ARE OVER, I AM FINALLY FLYING SOLO

There is a story line in the movie *The Shawshank Redemption* where James Whitmore, a lifetime prisoner, was released into society. He had been locked up for most of his life, and now he must reenter society. He did not want to be released because prison was the only way of life he knew. Such as it was, it was familiar to him. Against his will, he was released, and a short while after his release, they found he had hung himself. Although I did not entertain the idea of suicide, the first night I was alone after Ed moved his furniture, I understood how the released prisoner felt. I had never lived alone; such as it was, the marriage was my only way of life for twenty-seven of my forty-six years.

Like the character in the movie, I didn't know what to expect. I, too, was confined in a small emotional cell in the marriage for twenty-seven years. I'd been a mother for twenty-six of my forty-six years, and now the children had gone on their own. I no longer had the small business that fed my self-esteem.

As he stood at the exit gate, alone, with nothing but a few belongings, James Whitmore's character made me realize the intensity of my own feelings of aloneness and confusion. Then, when I saw the character hung himself out of despair, I knew I must hurry along and prepare an action plan that would give me direction and motivate me to move forward quickly before my feelings of despair took root.

I Think I Am Finally Free, Only to Begin a Different Struggle

It was final. The furniture was gone. I thought it was over. I thought I had finally corrected the error I made at the age of nineteen. I thought I was free. That was what I was thinking. I was thinking I would be free to do what I wanted. I would work hard and have some security, and finally, I would reclaim my life and choose the roads I wanted to travel toward my destiny. I didn't figure it would take me twenty years of struggling to correct the effects of the twenty-seven-year detour I took by staying married to Ed. I thought I was going to start over and move on in peace.

Once again, naive thinking!

First thing I did after Ed moved out, I went to see my mother. This time, I told her I was not seeking advice or opinions; I just came to tell her that I threw Ed out and that there was no turning back. I told her about some of his insane behaviors, and she told me she was aware of a few incidents, like the Wendy's incident with the sixteen-year-old and that he lost his job over it.

It was good to hear her say that if I confided in her with all the facts when I first drew up divorce papers in 1973, she would have helped me get that divorce. Of course that was water under the bridge. The sadness in her face is unforgettable. She spoke only a few words, but when our eyes met, we could both see that she inadvertently helped me replicate the life she had had with her father and her husband, Peter. That was the last time we discussed Ed or Peter. As I departed for Miami, I felt we both realized parenting does not lend itself to perfection; rather, it is based on life as it unfolds.

The First Week He Left, I Was Like Pavlov's Dog

It is not good to stay with a person that controls your life by fear. The longer you stay in such a relationship, the more the behavior of the controller permeates into every brain cell. This I know for sure. Once Ed moved out, every time I heard a car after dark, I thought the worst. At that time, my gun was like some sort of guard dog. Later in years, I realized I would have to rid myself of fear and not cling to my gun. One night, I said out loud, "It is better do be dead than live in fear." In time, I let go of the intensity of fear but never had been able to let go of the consciousness of fear. I still double bolt my doors the minute I come into my home.

Note to the Reader

If your life looks like mine, I send you love and power to reclaim your life.

The few times I saw Ed, he didn't plead to return home. Thank goodness! It seemed he moved on with the girlfriend he claimed he didn't have. I, on the other hand, was very happy he had someone else to use and manipulate. Despite all the evidence, he continued to taunt and, in my eyes, degrade me by telling everyone who was willing to listen, including my children and me, no less, that I made shit up all the time. A month or so after he moved out, I could take no more of his degrading. I promised myself, and I have kept that promise, that I would prove his lies with hard evidence and exit this marriage by handing off humiliation to him and his partner.

One evening, I went to his apartment. As I knocked on the door, I heard a lot of scurrying around, so I went to the back door. What did I see? As I approached the sliding door, there she was, the clever girlfriend, the loyal supervisor, the best friend, huddled like a childish imp or a convenience store robber in the bushes, half-dressed. All I could do was look at her in disgust. That was enough verification for me. He was a cheater, and she was his partner. I went into his apartment. Even though she was in the bushes, he acted as though she was not there. Can you imagine the audacity of such a liar? I saw her shoes in the trash basket. I took them out of the trash and threw them in the street. On the table, there was a romantic setup I had made for us for years. It consisted of a bottle of Seagram's Seven Crown, salami, and cheese and crackers. Can you imagine, between the two of them, they couldn't come up with anything original? These types of things can make a person laugh even when their heart is breaking.

While I was listening to Ed's lies, the girlfriend in the bushes hightailed it home. I had been humiliated by Ed and the likes of Bertha for twenty-seven years, and I was deadly determined that this was not how I was going to exit this marriage: labeled as a liar. At this point, I was determined with deadly resolve that no matter what, I was going to hand off the humiliation baton to Ed and Bertha forevermore.

Once I realized she departed, I forced him to call and have her return to his apartment while I was still there. In the past, when I had been in their presence, she paraded around like a peacock with colorful feathers. It was her turn to experience humiliation.

When she returned, I could only say, "You are the liars, not me." In that one moment, with that one short sentence, I took my power back! In that one moment, I promised myself that no one would ever dare to humiliate me again.

Twenty years have passed since, and I have kept my promise.

What Is Freedom?

When Ed moved out, I thought I was free. Now I was learning there are many tentacles to freedom. There is freedom from tyranny, there is financial freedom, there is emotional freedom, and so on. This moment was a defining moment for me. I knew right then from this experience that I had gained emotional freedom. Emotionally, I was free to move on, and I did.

How Did I Get Her to Come Back?

A cheater is a cheater. She was living with the man that threatened to use his guns if I came to her house. You may recall that this statement motivated me to purchase my gun. Perhaps he did not know of this special relationship between boss and subordinate. Their company did not allow fraternizing. I was using their crazy tactics. Perhaps they didn't know how far I would go with the anger they had instilled in me, just as I didn't know how far Ed would carry out his threats that I had feared for twenty-seven years. A bully is a coward, and for sure, they were cowards. Who knew why she came back.

Not long after this incident, I found out they were both fired from their positions at Pizza Hut, PepsiCo. Liars are cheaters, cheaters are thieves, and there are no limits to what they will steal. In their minds, their lies entitle them to all that they want, even if it belongs to others. By the way, I go on record that I had nothing to do with their getting fired.

Naïveté and Honesty

Looking back, I could see, although I was not perfect, I was a naive person with strong morals and sense of decency, and that made me an easy target for those who were not. When I am among dishonest people, decency still puts me at a disadvantage. I don't see a third option; I only see moral or immoral. I've learned to spot the liars and cheaters faster now, which has become my first line of defense. I have shed naïveté.

I am talking about these encounters to give the reader a sense of how cheaters and liars do not have a moral compass. Without a moral compass, they have no boundaries for what they do and what they say. I am also citing these encounters to let the reader know that sometimes—perhaps I should say initially—these encounters humiliate the innocent, but in the end, when turned on the cheaters, these encounters can also be liberating for the innocent. Cheaters are the most destructive human beings, especially to the honest and decent people. Tragically, for the people that care about them, they never change, because this is their way of life, not a matter of making a mistake. It is worth repeating for your sake and mine that if you live with a liar and a cheater, take the advice of the lady I met on my flight from Atlanta, who spoke softly and simply from her heart and experience when she said, "Dear, I don't know what is the matter, but if it is about a man, rid yourself of him as soon as you can." I swear that yesterday's woman, a stranger, gave me the best advice, but more importantly, she gave me a great sense of empowerment. If you need it, I pass on the empowerment to you.

Now We Find Out about Financial Freedom

Before I begin the story of the next twenty years after I separated from Ed, I must digress a little bit and give some background information that will lend clarity to the actions that followed.

Before we moved to Tampa, we purchased a condominium where the children could rest between school and roller-skating practice, because there wasn't always time to drive to our St. Petersburg home and the Tampa roller-skating arena where they practiced. When the children stopped roller-skating, we rented that condominium out as an investment while we lived in our town house. Ed was to collect the rent and pay the mortgage. We had $60,000 in the bank. One day, Ed, without letting me know, went to Miami and purchased a Jaguar using $40,000 of our savings. In hindsight, I should have seen this as a flag of what was to come. Sadly, I did not address this beyond an argument. Really, I should have transferred the rest of the money into a new savings account in my name.

While Ed was working at PepsiCo, he had great benefits, one of which was an excellent savings programs. PepsiCo would match the employee's savings—the percentage was based on the employee's salary. Ed was high in the management food chain, so this was a great benefit. If he put maximum percentage into savings, they would match the amount. We discussed this, and I agreed I would pay all the bills with my earnings and he would place the maximum amount allowed into that savings matching program. So essentially, what I am saying here is, I had no savings because I trusted a serpent like Ed, that the money we were saving was *our* joint retirement fund. Once again, I was naive. Sadly, twenty years ago, if a husband was dishonest, he could pull out all the money without the wife knowing. Thank goodness nowadays, in most companies, the wife must sign off when the husband tries to do that. Dear reader, if you don't know the policy of your spouse's retirement fund, make it your business to know it.

I knew when I was going to leave, so I began to prepare myself for the separation. For eight years, I owned a small consulting firm, Automation Control Inc. As in any small business, income had its peaks and valleys. I felt quite alone, so I knew I needed to find a position that offered a more stable income. To that end, I closed my business down and I accepted a position with Delta Airlines. By Ed's refusing to move to Texas or allowing me to move with the children, I was forced to quit American Airlines; thus, I had no retirement at all, except for what we saved in his retirement program.

I could not afford to stay in the big town house because the mortgage was beyond my current salary range. I knew I would have to give the house over to Ed. I didn't want to move out of the house until Erin was settled in college, so I postponed going to an attorney to file for divorce for a couple of months until Erin got settled at college. A big mistake!

Erin was determined to go to Gainesville for college with her girlfriends. I was worried and guilt ridden. I wanted her to stay in Tampa, where her sister and I were. After all, she was only seventeen. How could I say no to Erin when Raquel went to California at the similar age? I took all precautions. I insisted her friends' mother and I go to help the girls find an apartment, both mothers signed the lease, and school started. I was worried, but everyone reassured me it would all work out.

My friends worried about me being alone. One day, a friend insisted that I meet a man she worked with. I reluctantly agreed. It turned out the man was quite nice, well connected in the community. A corporate attorney. As I got to know Joe, I realized he seemed different from Ed. He was easygoing, was polite, and in appearance, was a kind man. His kindness totally lured me in. I was ready to move on, and with Joe's help, it seemed it would be easier, and in many ways, it was. I mention this meeting, and at this point, in some ways, I still feared Ed's wrath, but Joe's confidence and support gave me courage to file for my divorce. He helped me find an attorney.

It seemed I was moving forward. I made sure Erin was settled in school, and Raquel was living with her fiancé. I was settling in my new job with Delta Airlines. I met a nice man who seemed willing to be supportive. I thought the heavens had opened for my arrival. Not so fast!. Instead, I was pulled back through the doorway of hell.

First Meeting with My Attorney: Naïveté at Its Best

Nothing out of the ordinary during my initial meeting with the attorney. Short meeting. I told the attorney what I thought were our assets, all pertinent information, and stressed to my attorney that no matter how I felt, I wanted to be fair and split everything down the middle.

Second Meeting with My Attorney: Revelation

I thought this second meeting was for me to hear what was or wasn't mine and make my freedom official. Instead, it was like I was living the book of Revelation in the Bible. As he was talking, his words felt like someone was peeling my face. The pain and fear was taking me over. I asked the same questions over and over. The disbelief of his words rendered me unable to comprehend what he was saying.

I could barely sit still. He informed me that the investment condominium was in default. Apparently, my ex-husband-to-be had been collecting rent from the tenant and using the funds for his personal pleasure instead of paying the mortgage. To boot, at some point, the renters moved out and left the apartment uninhabitable. Ed pulled out all the money out of the bank and the retirement fund. He was not paying the mortgage on the townhome, and without the savings, I could not afford the mortgage with my existing salary. And since he had not been paying on the Jaguar, the Jaguar and the forty thousand he pulled out from our savings supposedly for the Jaguar were gone. After my divorce, I found out the Jaguar was a $60,000 car, and because he used our savings, he only owed $10,000 when it was repossessed. He didn't even bother to try to sell it to retrieve any money. All that was left was my seven-year-old BMW and Erin's car.

If all this wasn't enough, I found out from the attorney that Ed had been getting bonuses, which he never disclosed to me. That he used the bonus money for his own pleasure was one thing; however, I did the taxes, and not knowing about the bonuses, I never reported that money to the IRS. That he spent the money pissed me off, but that I did not report the money to IRS scared me.

I had a credit card in my name with a second user on the card for Raquel when she was in California, and my ex-husband ran the card up to $2,000. The card was in my name, and I didn't have the funds to pay his debt off.

As the attorney spoke, shock and dismay infected my brain. During my drive home, it sunk in that I had no home, no savings, no retirement fund, no credit, and that I owed the IRS.

By the time I arrived home, the shock and dismay had turned into enormous fear that I might never be able to overcome this travesty. How could my beginning and my end collide in such a way? Suddenly, I was afraid of both.

Third Meeting with My Attorney: Divorce Agreement

Now I understood the relationship between the hunter and the sitting duck

I liken my third meeting with my attorney to having surgery where the prognosis was good for surviving the surgery but the degree of handicap was uncertain. This time, the divorce papers were drawn and ready for signing. In the divorce agreement, I took possession of the condominium in default, my seven-year-old BMW, and Erin's car.

Ed was to pay back the IRS and my credit card that he ran up and take possession of the family townhome and pay me $700 a month in alimony.

Fourth Meeting with My Attorney: Signing the Divorce Papers

By this time, the divorce papers were ready for signatures. I was done crying. I had my combat boots on. I was coming out of shock and entering self-preservation mode. I decided, in order to keep my sanity, I must cut my losses and begin to focus on how I could start digging my way out of this hole. I signed the divorce papers, and Ed dragged his feet. He moved out of the state of Florida.

August 16, 1993 – one of my greatest infamies.

For the first time in my life, I knew pure rage! It is a feeling like no other when you realize another person annihilated your life and you feel helpless to do anything about it.

For my part, I just wanted this nightmare to be over. But no, liars and cheaters never stop. He was stalling. I threatened all kinds of things to get him to return to Florida to sign the divorce papers. This horrible man and this horrible woman, who taunted me for years, came to the attorney's office together to sign my divorce papers during the weekend they were celebrating her birthday. That was par for the course. At least I would get the papers signed so I could move forward. When I came in to collect the papers, I saw he signed the papers and felt relieved. As I looked over to the witness signature line, I saw her name, Bertha. No, I didn't only see her signature on the witness line; I also saw she was the witness on my divorce papers while celebrating her birthday!

When I saw her name and her birth date on what was to be my permanent document, I lost it. Dear God, I was sure my attorney must have thought I should be institutionalized. I for sure lost it. I was in such disbelief that they would stoop that low. I had to ask her description from the attorney a dozen times in different ways. I had enough. This was the last straw. Or so I thought. I left the attorney's office, and I called my mother. I called Ed, but I could not speak. All I could do was scream like a wounded animal. It was a moment in time that I can never forget. I can still hear my screaming in pain. I screamed like I was falling off a cliff. Pure rage! As I write this, I can still hear myself. I still wonder how someone can be that cruel. My rage was the culmination of twenty-seven years of struggling with the marriage, the outcome of the divorce, and now her signing my divorce papers while celebrating her birthday! My rage was intense. There were moments when I thought I'd gone insane and might not be able to find my way back.

At this juncture, every part of my life was destroyed or disrupted. Everywhere I turned, I saw nothing familiar. I had no home, I had no business, I had no money, and my children were on their own. I had no family structure. In my mind, I was like shattered glass; I couldn't see how I could put myself together and where to start. Later in years, I realized life is more like wood than glass. I was glad to move to that analogy, because glass shatters, while wood chips and can be repaired and made beautified again. Thankfully, I realized I was made of wood, not glass.

As time moved me along, I surmised God created friends and kindness to help people recover when they feel destroyed.

CHAPTER NINE

DREAMS AWAKEN HOPE, HOPE CAN MOVE MOUNTAINS

The irony: I was married on September 8, 1966, and I was divorced on September 8, 1993.

As I was coming out of the courtroom on September 8, 1993, all I could think and feel was that a great, dark cloud was removed from my mind; a great weight was lifted off my shoulders. Once again, I dared to be optimistic and feel I was free to feel, do, and achieve anything I wanted. I immediately started planning my recovery, emotional and financial.

I had to give up the townhome, as stated in the divorce agreement, so there was a matter as to where I was going to live. The investment condominium was in default, and it was trashed. I called my mother and finally told her what was happening. She was extremely understanding. She lent me money to take the condominium out of default and to clean it up. God will bless her for that.

September and October passed. I was making progress, until suddenly, I started getting calls from creditors. As I mentioned earlier, Ed moved out of the state of Florida, and for that reason, they couldn't find him. Instead, they found me. He took no action on the divorce agreement. The creditors had been mailing notices to him, and he simply ignored them all, so by the time the creditors turned to me, it was all do or die, especially the IRS.

He sent no alimony payments. I did not pursue it. I was full of dismay, and Ed's threats still lingered in the back of my mind. I had so many things to overcome I felt his reaction would be just one too many. I was not to receive my alimony until five years after the divorce, at which point I was ready to overcome the hurdle of fearing Ed. I hired an attorney to collect my current alimony and the back pay for the previous five years. He owed me $42,000 in back payments. The attorney was going to force him to pay me the full amount, and foolishly, I prevented him; instead, I just asked for $100 a month on top of the amount due me, once again for fear of his reprisal. And rightly so.

The day he received the attorney papers requiring him to pay my alimony, he sent Bertha's (you remember Bertha, the girlfriend) son to break the windows of my car. My car was parked just a few feet outside my neighbor's and my bedroom windows, and as soon as we heard running, we were on alert. By the time they broke my first window, my neighbor and I were outside. We could easily make out the boys' faces, clear as day. I recognized Bertha's son, but not his friend. I read previously in the newspapers that this boy was already in trouble with the law. I told my neighbor I would not report the incident; I didn't want to get tangled up with Ed and with a child who was capable of being influenced by someone like Ed and doing such an act. Believe it or not, he still owed me alimony, and at the rate he was paying me, it would take twenty years for him to pay me the amount he owed. I must live to be eighty-nine years old to collect what he owes me. If it weren't so mean-spirited, it would be comical.

I received notice from the credit card company that they were canceling my credit card. This was the only credit card I had. I received a notice from the mortgage company demanding payment or repossession of the property. Apparently, our laws state that if Ed sold the house and made a profit, I would not be entitled to the profit; however, because I was on the mortgage papers, even though the divorce papers stated the property was his, if they couldn't find him, I was still liable for the mortgage. My dumb-ass lawyer never told me that.

As soon as I realized what was happening, I consulted the attorney, and he suggested bankruptcy. I filed for bankruptcy thinking I would be permanently removed from Ed's share of debt, and ultimately, I was, but not for the IRS.

The bankruptcy court permits a person to keep a residence and one car. Sadly, I was on two car titles, my car and Erin's. There was no way to explain to bankruptcy court that my daughter Erin worked and saved to purchase this car. I was on the title because she was a minor when she purchased it. To keep her car, I had to relinquish mine.

A week before Thanksgiving, the IRS garnished my wages. I was incensed. I thought I would do something bad. I called Ed, and honestly, at this juncture, if he did not pay the IRS right, then I might be writing this book from the penitentiary, because I had had enough of these jolts. My emotions were battered for twenty-seven years, and I could take no more. Not only was I going on my own for the first time, but I was also broke and forced to go through bankruptcy because of this crazy, irresponsible man. During this one conversation, not only did I believe I was capable now of doing him great harm; I also got the feeling he finally believed it. He paid the IRS, and they released my paycheck.

So I lost once again. I went through bankruptcy to clear myself of Ed's end of the debts while he enjoyed all the money from our savings and retirement fund and lived in a big house on the golf course. Where is the justice in that?

Here I was, no money, no credit, no car, but I was loaded with faith that God would continue to send messengers my way to guide me. And he did.

Friends helped me clean up and paint the condominium. I moved in and began the climb out of the financial and emotional hole. I vacillated between calm, strong, and hopeful and shattered, fearful, and heartbroken.

At this time, I was working for Delta Airlines, in one of their automation departments. Delta was a great airline to work for. During my brief tenure there, I met several excellent peers, and some became lifelong friends. Their advice and friendship were immeasurable when I needed them the most. Shortly after my divorce and bankruptcy was final, I received a call from the senior vice president at American Airlines. That was not too unusual because I received several such calls from him when I had my operations consulting business. He would call to inquire if I would visit a client of his and help with the operational efficiencies. But this call was a little different in that he wanted me to meet with the vice president of air and sea operations at Royal Caribbean Cruises. I explained I no longer did consulting, that I was an employee at Delta. Royal Caribbean Cruises was one of the Delta's and American's biggest clients. Not so mysterious. After I met with the RCCL vice president, both Delta and American agreed I should take the job offer from Royal Caribbean. Taking this job offer meant I would have to move to Miami. I wasn't sure about taking on another transition, but I was strapped financially. The RCCL salary would be almost double of what I was making at Delta, so I took the job. I must say, this was a huge blessing and one of the most productive decisions I had ever made, for many reasons. The salary, the environment, and the people I met there were heaven-sent.

I am excited to tell the story about the first official meeting with the RCCL vice president, Margarita. I drove up to the RCCL offices located in Miami, right on the water. Along the office building was this huge ship. I felt like I was a little ant next to it. I walked in with awe and said to the VP, "Oh, Margarita, the boat is magnificent!"

With a firm voice, she said to me, "Anita, if you are in the boat, the ship is sinking."

I called that huge ship a boat.

I love that story. She was the most gracious and classy executive I had ever met, and in my business, I worked with many executives. She was a tough taskmaster and a kind heart at the same time. During the first meeting, she informed me of her expectations. One such expectation was that I might on occasion have to travel. I would use my credit card, and the company would reimburse my expenses. And here it started again, remnants of Ed's betrayal. I decided to come clean. I pulled out my divorce and bankruptcy papers to help me explain why I could not have a credit card. I pointed to the right column on the divorce paper that was my ex-husband's responsibility and explained he left the state and defaulted on all his responsibilities, which redirected the creditors to me because I was local. I continued that that situation caused me to go through bankruptcy to clear myself of his share of debts. At the same time, I eyed that horrible cheater-woman's signature on the witness line of my divorce paper. The shame and humiliation was too much, and I lost my composure. As she saw I was fighting tears, this most gracious woman said to me something like this: "Not too many escape divorce. Don't worry, we can fix everything." She was on the board of directors of one of the financial institutions in Miami. She picked up the telephone and called to arrange for my visit to prepare applications. She said, "While you are there, why don't you open a local checking account?" My heart was pounding. First, the doubling of my salary and, now, the helping with my credit situation. At the same time, I was thinking, *Mercy, I have $26 until l receive my last paycheck from Delta or first paycheck from RCCL.* Either way, I was going to eat soup and crackers for a few days. I didn't know why, if it was the norm or I was a lucky person that day, but Margarita put me up at the Marriot in Miami for a month and gave me my moving expense in advance. There was nothing I could say to describe my gratitude and respect for this excellent woman.

If all this was not enough, heaven sent me the dearest couple in the world as my guardians, Omar and Casandra. I know there is a special place in heaven for them. The minute Margarita introduced me to Casandra, I felt safe. She and her husband, Omar, helped me find a furnished one-bedroom apartment, and when I moved out of there, they protected me when the landlord tried to swindle me out of my deposit. During the years I lived in Miami, these two were like my brother and sister. And they still are. They helped me move four times, helped me find new apartments, and finally, helped me purchase a condominium, which ultimately made me some money when I sold it. As long as I lived in Miami, I was never lonely because of them. Casandra and Omar and Casandra's parents were kind and welcoming. They often included me in their family dinners. When I would get crazy about all the changes I had had to endure, Casandra would calm me down, always having some kind words, something like "That too shall pass" or something like "What goes around comes around, Annie." I couldn't always accept her encouragement because, adding insult to injury, Ed and his accomplice returned to Tampa and purchased a big house on the golf course while I struggled to pay for food. I was still waiting for "what goes around" to come around, but I was much more patient then because Casandra had convinced me that just because I didn't see the "come around" didn't mean it wouldn't or didn't happen. I accepted that.

By now it was apparent even to me that my existence was like a yo-yo, up and down at every turn. Down with despair and worry and up with elation and progress.

After a year and a half with RCCL, the VP of American Airlines called me again. Apparently, the RCCL vice president felt I had accomplished my reorganization mission. He convinced me to accept a job with American Airlines to look at his Latin and Central reservations and ticketing office operations, to see what improvements could be made. I enjoyed the pleasure of traveling to all the Latin and Central American countries. There was so much to learn and enjoy. Those who managed the American Airlines stations were hardworking and gracious people. Although at times the work and travel were grueling, it was enlightening. The position was rewarding financially and in rebuilding my self-image and dignity.

Joe, the Last Straw

At the same time, while I was working in Miami, I continued to date Joe. I commuted from Miami to Tampa for five years. I marveled at the fact that every weekend, I drove four and a half hours each way back and forth from Miami to Tampa. Now, when I look back, it seemed simply insane that I did that commute. What made it more insane was, I was the only one doing it. That should have been a red flag. Aaaah, my dear friend, hindsight, comes to mind.

Joe did not sacrifice his time and convenience to help with the commute. When I came in for the weekend, Joe had everything arranged. He would call me to see how close I was to the house, and when I was pulling in the driveway, he would start my bathwater so I could take a bath, whether I wanted one or not. He made arrangements when, where, and with whom we would have dinner, where we would go, etc. He had a desk job, and so it was hard for him to take a leap and consider that working all week in Argentina, Brazil, or Venezuela and flying or driving to Tampa might be exhausting. He had his agenda, and that was what we followed.

The first weekend I missed going to Tampa, Joe tried to tell me he was lonely. Instead of coming to Miami to see me, he called to tell me that because I did not come for the weekend, he met an old friend and spent the weekend with her. After his many apologies, flowers, and changing of story, I accepted his apology. I let this big warning flag go!

A cheater is a cheater. Even after they divorce the first wife for cheating, they don't change.

About five years into this relationship, Joe was pressuring me to quit my job and return to Tampa for us to get married. And I did that insane thing again: I quit my job and moved back to Tampa, with the intention to marry Joe. It took me only a few months after living with Joe to begin feeling stifled by his control. Dear me! I traded in one control freak for another. In time, I realized I almost overcorrected my error with Ed. I divorced a loud controller and traded him in for a seemingly soft-spoken, better-manipulating controller. Worse, I began to panic like crazy when I realized what I was about to go into, a *marriage*. He wanted me to contribute to household expenses. He wanted me to sign a prenuptial agreement. He wanted me to live in a house that was in his name only while, at the same time, he wanted me to contribute to the mortgage payment. I offered to match the down payment he had on the house, and thus we would jointly own the house, but he stalled until it was apparent he was not going to allow equality. I saw too many red flags. Essentially, when all is said and done, what all this was adding up to if we married and either divorced or Joe was to die first was, I would be booted out of the house by his family and be penniless and homeless in my old age. The summation of what Joe wanted further hardened me against marriage.

This experience was the final straw. I saw marriage only as a prison—desolate, lonely, controlling, and hard to get out of. This feeling was branded in my heart, and I knew, going forward, I would never be able to step into marriage again.

To make matters worse, I could not find a job. At this juncture, I had an excellent professional reputation with experience in high-ranking positions of responsibility, which I accomplished without a college degree. I went for a few months without getting a single résumé call or job interview. I was beginning to lose my self-confidence. My work was closely aligned with my self-image and my achievements. Now, two-thirds of my life was out of control.

Finally, I asked friends who were in human resource positions what was happening. And then there it was! I was told companies did not even look at résumés if the candidates did not have a college degree, especially for high-ranking positions. More time passed, and each week my sense of urgency to leave Joe grew. More and more my life with Joe started to look like my life with Ed.

One day, I woke up as the sun was rising and prepared a plan to leave Joe.

Note to Girls, Young and Old: Always Have a Plan

First thing I had to do was find a job, any job. I also resolved to get a college degree. The second thing I had to do was get my own place to live. Being fifty-four years old added a sense of urgency to move forward. Next day, after I made my resolve to leave Joe, I searched the newspapers for job postings. I saw an ad posted by Chase Manhattan Bank for entry-level jobs. The posting said that for starting positions, college assistance was possible. I didn't care what job they were interviewing for; I was not going to leave until they gave me a job. It was all crazy. I had to interview with three different people to get an entry-level position. They worried that I was overqualified and the pay was low. Lord, both of those things were true; entry-level job and $25,700 annual pay. As the saying goes, I was an executive-level employee making almost three times that amount. I explained to all the people at Chase who talked to me that a low-paying job was much better than no job, and their educational program was priceless to me. I assured them, with my experience, they would most likely want to promote me in six to eight months. As I predicted, I was promoted to quality assurance manager after six months, and Chase paid for my bachelor's degree in psychology, human development.

Same day, right after I took the job with Chase, I drove a couple of miles down the road from Chase to a condominium community where my daughter Raquel and her husband lived. I loved that community. I especially loved this one condo because from the patio one could see the boat dock. In front of the boat dock, there was a small island that was visible only when the water receded with the tide. Something urged me on to move to that community. Nervously, I walked up to the condo that was in front of the small island and knocked on the door. An elderly lady answered. I prefaced my question with a little story. I said that I had just taken a job offer down the street after a long divorce recovery and I would find her condominium most suitable for my healing. I asked her if she could contemplate the possibility of selling her condo in the near future. I pulled out my check and added, "I can give you $40,000 deposit today if you would like to consider the sale."

She responded sweetly, "I will check with my husband and get back to you. Will you wait, please?"

When I heard her say *wait, please,* elation took me over. As I waited, I was excited she didn't say no, and at the same time, I worried that maybe she was calling the police. After all, although sincere, my approach was a bit odd. After a short wait, the elderly lady invited me in to talk with her husband and her daughter. I left my check, and the sale was arranged. What good fortune! Their daughter was a real estate closing agent. In two weeks, I closed the sale, and in three weeks, I moved into the wonderful condominium, and my soul moved into nature's arms.

I Could Not Believe My Good Fortune— It Was Like Riding on a Cloud

In one day, I got a job and purchased my home!

There might be something to the saying "Ask and you shall receive." Once again, in one day, my life changed completely. I moved out of Joe's house, I started a new job at Chase, and I started accelerated courses at Eckerd College. I was crazy in the other direction now. I could not believe my good fortune. If I believed in God, prayer, and God's messengers before, now that belief became unshakable. I said to myself out loud, "God is good, and hope is an eternal optimist."

College was the most magnificent thing I did for myself. I deliberately chose psychology for my degree and human development for my subject. When I moved in to my new condominium, I would sit on the patio, look out to the water, and cry. Although I did not feel lonely, I felt great aloneness. I think it was at this juncture that I grew to feel that we are never alone; a certain spirit exists in us and around us, and if we sit still, we can feel it. After a while, I could also see it. Each day I observed the water's ebb tide. When the water receded, I could see my island, and when the water returned, the island was covered with water. I began to see how nature breathes, and in time, I went out on the patio to breathe with nature, not to cry.

I felt I was pretty broken and did not know how to fix myself. I could see things were improving, but I didn't have the skills to diminish the pain and fears I had accumulated in the previous thirty years. I couldn't enjoy the good things that were happening because, like Pavlov's dog, I was always waiting for the other shoe to drop. I took to school with a vengeance, searching for answers. I went to school days, nights, and weekends. I studied all night when I had to. I graduated in less than two years, and I was fifty-five years old. By graduation, I learned how to put the pieces of my life in proper order, which memories to lock away and which to rejoice in. This was the beginning of living my life.

My Mother, Vera

As I write this section, my heart is filled with regret that I did not make more time to visit with my mother before she died.

When I returned to Tampa to marry Joe, I was in pretty good shape financially. I think Vera was pleased to see me move forward. I was grateful to her for the help she gave me after my divorce. During our conversations, she conveyed she was glad I gave her that opportunity. Her life with Roy never reached a peaceful indifference, as sometimes old people who don't love each other reach. I would visit her when I would come in town, and she was always sad. Three years after my divorce, she complained about having the flu for several weeks. I urged her to see the doctor, but like many Serbians, we didn't see doctors for healing; we saw them when we were desperately ill. And that was what my mother did. I could see she was not well, and so I urged her to see a doctor every time I saw her. When she finally did see the doctor, it was too late. She was diagnosed with terminal leukemia, and she was told she would not live more than six months. We tried to match bone marrow, but at her age and the stage of her disease, those treatments were not an option. I couldn't accept the news. I felt I could do something more.

I talked to the senior vice president at American Airlines, and he suggested some of the best doctors in Miami. I decided to take her with me to Miami for treatments. The drive to Miami was over four hours. I was concerned, so I stopped at her hospital for her to have one last blood transfusion. I was optimistic. I thought I could take care of her, to help her find peace, but it was not meant to be. While I was waiting for her to complete her transfusion, she would look up in the ceiling and talk to someone. I was fearful, because in our nationality, we have certain mores about death. One is that someone comes to get us on our journey to heaven. I was panicked, pleading with her not to talk to whoever it is, to tell them to wait, that we were going for new treatments. My pleading was to no avail. For thirty minutes, she would ask me every few minutes what time it was, and she would ask me to leave and come back later. The more she asked me to leave, the more the terror in me increased. Finally, she did not ask me to leave; she insisted that I leave her for an hour. I knew if I left, she would die. I knew that from the old yesterday's women's stories and from her conversations with me. I had to leave, though. Those were the spiritual rules. When I returned in half an hour, they shut the door and told me she had passed.

She and I had gone through a lot of pain, hers and mine. I pray that she is happy where she is, because she deserves happiness. She has earned it.

In later years, I've come to a realization that the cruel parallels between her life and mine were not out of something we did; it was something that we allowed others to do to us. At every turn, Roy and Peter threw a bomb in her world and created wounds with each one, as did Ed in mine. In retrospect, I see now each of us could have left our spineless captors, control freaks, but we did not, out of some sense of obligation we felt to everyone around us except to ourselves. That was the weakness we had in common. I begged her so many times to buy a nice condominium for herself and enjoy friends, but she would never leave the home. At least I set a deadline to leave my situation, but she never did. She thought if she stayed, she could preserve the wealth she had accumulated for the children. Sadly, she died in her unhappiness, and some other woman and not her children were enjoying the wealth she had worked hard and sacrificed for.

For many years, I would visit her on Sundays, and she would read my tea leaves. I believed she knew what she told me. I still do. I miss those moments when she and I were together, bonding over something enjoyable that Roy or Ed could not destroy or penetrate. In the end, we were each other's caregivers.

Seek to Understand Your Mother, It Will Help You Understand Yourself

I understood myself better as I came to understand my mother. As I revisited my past, I came to realize some of my strengths to endure came from her inner strength and experience. She constantly grew, she cared about her family, and she endured Roy. It was not until today that I connected that I unknowingly separated my life in those three categories: my personal growth, my children, and my struggles with my relationships with Ed and Joe.

Roy and Peter

When Roy and Vera came to the United Sates, they were just two immigrants with two suitcases. They worked hard. Vera worked around-the-clock and ultimately made her children do the same. That was the foreigner's way. She saved every penny she could. One year, she took a vacation with friends and fell in love with a little sixteen-unit motel in St. Petersburg and bravely purchased it. Roy was against it, but then Roy was against anything that might cause him work. She worked around-the-clock, washed the sheets, cleaned the rooms, and managed the motel rental and financial activity. Eventually, they added a second story onto this small motel. The business thrived. She made the motel a home for the snowbirds, especially, and as her business grew, she did not stop there—she continued to save, which ultimately enabled her and Roy to purchase a 150-unit hotel. When they sold the motel, they invested in nineteen townhomes near the ocean.

When Vera died, there was no will for their estate. The estate was estimated approximately 2.3 million. My half-sister, Zorica, and I knew her father, Roy, was an illiterate man in any language, and her brother, Zoran, was a hopeless drug addict. Zoran died from drug overdose in the back seat of a police car three years after Vera died. He was forty-two years old. With this knowledge, Zorica and I decided to place all the properties into a trust, which would protect the properties from outside intruders.

One day, about a year or so after Mother's death, Roy came to me and Zorica and informed us he had married his housekeeper, a Bulgarian woman. On his deathbed, he confided in me that he was sorry and that he made a very grave mistake getting married without our knowledge. But his cleansing confession was meaningless. It was all too late. At that time, I was still dating Joe, who was an attorney. He gave me a heads-up that this woman would get everything as his wife if the trust fund was broken. I shared that information with Zorica, and she reassured me that the trust was intact. After his funeral, we were told by Roy's attorney that everything belonged to Peppi, the Bulgarian wife, and her children, that we could get nothing, not even personal things that belonged to our mother. Yes, my sister allowed the trust fund to be broken. I never discussed why she did it; I only knew greed is a viscous animal. At least my sister got some money when the trust was broken. I did not get a dime.

My justification for staying in a bad marriage for twenty-seven years was for the sake of the children, and Vera's justification was the same. She felt that if she divorced, some other woman would enjoy the fruits of her labor, and if she stayed, she could control the wealth. Lord have mercy, some other woman is indeed enjoying the fruits of her labor as we speak. What do we call this travesty?

I Took a Pause from Writing

It has been a week since I wrote chapter 8. I debated with myself during this week if I should discuss the effects of recalling the events and the pain I experienced. I decided to share my mental state during and after the writing of the last two chapters, which I found to be traumatic and cleansing at the same time. Many emotions surfaced and spilled into my soul. At times, I was angry. At times, I was sad. At times, I was joyful. Mostly, I was sorry I squandered my youth by allowing Ed to control my existence. I was sorry I did not take time to understand my mother's plight from the perspective of helping her, because as I was writing, I realized I wouldn't have freed myself either without the dear, kind friends who gave me a push and support to do so. All along, I thought I was her lifeline, yet while writing, I realized we were each other's lifeline. I searched my mind as I had many times in the past, asking, did I let her down by not packing her up and removing her from Roy sooner? I know now I could not commandeer her life. I recalled my daughters telling me the same thing I told Vera, to leave their father sooner, yet

I, too, had my reasons that I did not. At that time, they seemed like good reasons. Now the reasons look like I squandered my opportunities for happiness.

I recalled the questions posed to me by my daughters, who, in some ways, felt the way I did about my mother: why didn't I leave sooner? This question was painful to hear as it echoed in my mind because it just validated that they did not, and still do not, realize the great sacrifices I made to stay and why. By mid-chapter, I was feeling anxious, and by the end of the chapter, I began experiencing chest pains. With each paper I pulled out of my files to verify the information I was writing about, my heart began to pound. The rhythm was off. I stopped writing. I paced. I tried to calm down. Hours later, I talked to a friend, and she encouraged me to call a doctor, which was what I did. I believe the longer we stay in pain, the more it becomes an imprint in our heart, like an etching on a piece of wood. If you stay long enough, you become more comfortable in the state of pain than the unknown possibilities of knowing happiness. Reentering the pain-filled chambers of my mind and placing the memories in the light of the written pages felt truly traumatic. Anxiety took me over.

Note to Women, Young and Old

I press on, hoping the lessons I have learned and share with you will enlighten and encourage you to trust in your courage and the capacity you have to do what is necessary to fill your life with peace and joy. A stranger once told me that it is obligatory to seek joy. The following is my conversation with the yesterday's woman who gave me this wisdom.

When we first found out my mother had leukemia, we waited for the test results to find out how far along her illness had progressed. My sister lived in California and I lived in Florida, and for that reason, I was the designated person to talk to the doctor and then explain to my mother and Roy, in Serbian, what the situation was.

It was late in the day. I was sitting at the Miami airport. I had just arrived from Brazil and was waiting for a flight to Tampa when I received the call from my mother's doctor. After proper identification exchanges, I heard the doctor say, "The leukemia is extremely advanced." I was sitting among many people, so I tried to stay composed. I asked the doctor what could be done to help her, and his reply was, because of the stages of the leukemia and my mother's age—she was sixty-six years old—there wasn't much that could be done. Without my asking, the doctor volunteered, "She has about six months to live." I, of course, did not believe that. I believed hope can move mountains. As I found out at the end of the six months, hope cannot defeat leukemia.

While I was struggling with the doctor's words, I felt suspended in space, out of my body, floating in pain. Suddenly, the word *reeling* made sense, for I felt I was reeling, like the suspended feeling you get during a car accident. I tried to stay calm. I decided not to call anyone until I arrived in Tampa, and there I would have a better footing on the situation.

Finally, I was on my flight to Tampa. I had locked my seat belt for takeoff when the stewardess tapped me on the shoulder and asked me to move back a couple of rows. Of course I complied. As I settled into my seat once again, the elderly lady next to me, very well-groomed, with great poise, began to speak to me. She said, "I asked the stewardess to move you next to me." She continued, "Dearie, I noticed the change in your face when you received a call while waiting to board the plane. Your spirit sent out such a message of distress that I feel compelled to comfort you." I was taken aback by her observation and subsequent kind words. I told her of my news, and she explained to me that she understood how I felt. Her son was designated to tell her she had cancer a few years earlier. She understood my pain, especially because I would be the one to discuss the news with my mother. After several minutes into our conversation, she closed with a statement that I have recalled many times to remind me I must keep working at making my life better. She said, "I am a Jewish woman. In my religion, we believe it is obligatory to seek joy in our life." I hope she is blessed wherever she is. That was a kind message that helped me pull through many painful tunnels.

God, I Need Help

You know how when something is happening, we don't know whom to turn to, so we look up into the heavens and cry out loud, "God, I need help." Throughout my hardships and joyful times, I have come to accept the idea that strangers are God's messengers he sends to direct and, when necessary, to lift us up and, when we are happy, to share our joy.

Be open, my dear reader. A stranger may be delivering a message to you.

CHAPTER TEN

ORDER OUT OF CHAOS

I graduate from college, with honors, 2003.

I am ready to put the puzzle together of who I am to become.

When I started college in 2001, I was fifty-four years old. I was like a runaway train. I was moving as fast as I could to recover financially and emotionally. In my mind, being fifty-four years old and emotionally shattered created an even greater urgency to fix both. Looking for goodness in my life was like looking for delicate flowers in a garden overrun by tall prickly cactus. I was grateful for my job at Chase and my new condominium. I was learning to sit still on the patio and watch nature breathe. I was learning to breath with nature.

But that was all outside of my soul.

Inside, I had no continuity, no confidence that my present peace and progress would last. My mind was like a box full of puzzle pieces. I longed to put the pieces together so that I could see how life would look for me as I worked on rebuilding myself. Whom could I turn to for help? To teach me how to help myself, where to start, how to determine what was broken and what was strong and peaceful in me? My yesterday's woman was gone. I couldn't see the good in me for the evil deeds I experienced. I realized I was too complicated for friends to direct me. They, too, felt helpless as they watched my despair and joy teeter-totter through my life thus far. Up and down. They knew their advice was limited to what they could observe and what I expressed to them. I appreciated their encouragement, but I feared their advice was abstract, limited by what I did not express and what they did not observe. I knew, I had to find a way to bring order out of the chaos that existed in my mind.

My Path from Chaos to Order

After intensely pondering what I should do, I concluded the best course of action would be to seek a degree in psychology with a focus on human development. I felt this education would expose me to developmental psychologists and psychoanalysts known for their theory on psychosocial development of human beings and psychosocial developmental patterns. It is safe to say this decision might have saved my sanity; at the very least, it helped me bring order out of chaos.

I took to college like a starving person takes to food. I took three to four accelerated courses at a time while working full-time. I worked and studied with very little time in between for rest. At times, I would write assignment papers so intense the professors would call me in for counseling. Their advice was timely and enlightening.

Early on in my studies, I looked for classes that would discuss developmental stages from a psychosocial perspective, so I was thrilled when I was introduced to Erikson's theory. Erikson's theory was a perfect tool for me to solve my life's puzzle. It was an organized and easy-to-comprehend theory, which was what I desperately needed. In his theory, Erikson believed eight stages of psychosocial development unfold as we go through our life span. Each stage consists of a unique developmental task that confronts individuals with a turning point that must be faced. Perfect, I thought. I would sort and align my garbled life's experience with his stages. Right away, I began to sort my chaotic experiences within the parameters of Erikson's stages, one at a time. I worked intensely for over a year to identify and sort my life's experiences and align them with Erikson's stages. I went to Europe several times to meet with my brother and sisters, with my aunt, with my school friends before I came to the United States, with my parents' friends, and so on. I visited places that jarred my memories—old smells, old sceneries, customs, and mores. I spoke in my native language, went to authentic Serbian Orthodox churches, blended in with Serbian ways and pace of living, and more.

I was armed with a lifetime of information; all I needed to do now was place it in some order. I used Erikson's stages as a tool to help me create order out of chaos. Per his theory, the first four stages unfold from infancy up to ten years of age. During this developmental period, children learn trust versus distrust, autonomy/independence versus shame and doubt, Initiative versus guilt, and industry versus inferiority. As I was learning about all the stages, I began to identify events that validated each stage. Erikson's belief was that each turning point offers an enhanced potential. The more the individual resolves the crises successfully, the healthier the development will be. As I moved through this process, I realized that I had favorably resolved my changes during this span from infancy to ten years of age. This realization began to build warmth and calm inside me. When I left Serbia, I felt strongly I could trust everyone I knew there—my grandmother, my grandfather, my aunt, my siblings, my parents' childhood friends. The trust for them led me to think the world was a good and pleasant place to live.

I recalled my feelings of independence when my brother and sisters and I went on the train to the family farm. I recalled funny examples of my initiative and enthusiasm about learning. For example, when I wanted to see a set of baby ducks in a muddy area with my new Sunday outfit after my uncle said not to do it, my initiative constantly brought me in contact with a wealth of new adventures. I recalled my teacher Zlata coercing me into the adventure of learning things that I would never have thought of by myself, which eventually gave me courage to take initiative to try and create things on my own. I recalled how industrious my sister and I were; we didn't have dolls, so we created them out of matchsticks, thread, and a little bit of material for their clothing. Silly but warm memories. I was on my way. I pulled out the events of the first four stages of my development and organized them in line with Erikson's stages, and I was satisfied that I found a way to bring my life's experience into a manageable and enjoyable format, one that I could look back on and with which I could enjoy the good things I enjoyed and put away the unhappy events where they would not be mixed with the good. I began to build peace within me with each memory or conversation. My childhood was safe, and I was once again safe in it. I validated this feeling each year I got together with my brother and sisters.

The remaining four stages were also separated by turning points that consisted of a unique developmental task and age span. For example, one dealt with identity versus identity confusion in stage 5, at the age of ten to twenties; with intimacy versus isolation in stage 6, at the age of twenty to thirty; with generativity versus stagnation in stage 7, at the age of forty to fifty; and in stage 8, at the age of sixty until death, with integrity versus despair.

I was happy to learn that some of my crises were part of normal human development, while others were enhanced by the lack of support from my mother and husband, who were going through their own crises. In stage 5, while I was trying to determine my identity to find out who I was, what I was about, and where I was going in life, my mother and husband were going through their own identity crisis, which caused them to interfere with mine rather than support me in my search.

As I continued to sort my experiences and organize them in categories and age spans, I was amazed how well my life stages matched with Erikson's. When I finished with my sorting, I found Erikson's theory most comforting, especially his belief that each stage consists of a unique developmental task that confronts individuals with a crisis that must be faced. I was calmed when he clarified this crisis is not a catastrophe but a turning point of increased vulnerability and enhanced potential. During this process, it became apparent to me that I had resolved many more crises successfully than I realized. Also, I could see the difference between turning points in my life and crisis where I had no control. I realized also that while I was going through my stage 5, identity versus identity confusion, so was Ed. However, in our case, instead of giving each other love and support, his explorations and relationships outside our home added more burden to my task of trying to find out who I was and where I was going in life.

While applying Erikson's theory, I also learned a great deal about others in my life, mainly Vera. I learned that at the same time I was going through my crisis with my life and Ed, my mother couldn't see the forest for the trees, as the saying goes. She was only thirty-seven years old when I was nineteen. While I was going through my identity crisis (stage 5), she was going through intimacy versus isolation (stage 6). To achieve intimacy, one must form healthy friendships and intimate relationships. I realize now that was not possible for her to achieve; she could not replace the loss of her beloved mother and friend, and she was left with two thoughtless men, Peter and Roy, who hindered her progress in this direction all the days of her life.

As I learned how to use Erikson's theory as my tool, I slowly established my identity. However, I still found myself at the crossroads of intimacy versus isolation (stage 6). Then one day in 1998, my first grandson, Jake, was born. My goodness! The minute I saw this little boy's sweet, tiny face, I was in love with him instantly. My heart opened like a great, big white flower. With each day, his unconditional love, sweet smile, and affection filled my heart with joy. His sweetness taught me to love and trust again. He is nineteen now, and to this day, when I see him, he fills my heart with joy. I have six grandsons now, and because of the healing I experienced from Jake's warm smile and unconditional love, as only a child can give, I can and do bask in the love of every one of my sweet, loving grandsons. They are what joy is all about.

By the time I graduated from college, I was fifty-six years old, well into Erikson's generativity versus stagnation (stage 7). According to Erikson, in this stage, a chief concern is to assist the younger generation in developing and leading useful lives. I was comfortable in this stage. As I examined my life through the prism of this stage, I realized I was finally satisfied with my life's foundation, with my identity, and with intimacy. I knew I had a lot to offer, and I liked sharing my knowledge with the younger generation. While in this stage, I became a guardian ad litem and a case manager as an advocate for abused and neglected children.

I am now in Erikson's eighth and final stage of development. Without Erikson's stage 8, we may call this the retirement stage, but I like his integrity versus despair contrast. As I entered this stage, I realized, I am reflecting on the past and piecing together a review and concluding if my life has been well spent. Though I have taken many different routes, I have developed a positive outlook in most of all the previous stages of development. My retrospective glances reveal a picture of a life well spent. As a person, I feel a sense of satisfaction. I feel I have reached integrity.

CHAPTER ELEVEN

KNOWLEDGE AFTER COLLEGE

I don't think I learned many new things about life while in college. However, what I did learn was invaluable. I learned how to harness my emotions. I learned how to sort the good experiences from the bad and joy from pain. Before this knowledge, all my experiences, good and bad, were mixed together, which caused me to live in constant pain and anxiety. I was angry with myself all the time for eloping, for staying with Ed out of fear and for the sake of the children, for allowing him to sever me from my career, for my tolerating his indiscretions, for allowing others to control my existence—all of it. The day I wore my cap and gown and my honor medallion, I let go of my anger and gave myself a clean slate. From my graduation day forward, I took to living my life on my own terms. I've kept my word to myself: no one gets to humiliate or control me.

I loved working for Chase, and I was most fortunate they paid for my college degree. In 2005, Chase management informed us that they were expanding in Mumbai, India. I, among several other employees, was asked if I would volunteer to go to India to train the new employees. I was elated to go.

Another fabulous experience. Within six weeks of our return, Chase sent out notices that they were closing the Tampa offices. They lied—they weren't expanding their business; instead, they were moving the offices to India. Everyone was laid off.

In my field of study, I was required to do internship. To fulfill this requirement, I became a guardian ad litem, an advocate for abused and neglected children. The requirement was one semester. I stayed on for seven years. It was a very challenging and rewarding experience. Because of this experience, I became a case manager for abused and neglected children, a wrenching, daunting job. There is no way not to love every one of those children. The system is as flawed as the parents that abuse the children. I left after being a case manager a year because the only thing I was accomplishing was endangering myself and giving the children false hope when they grew to love me. I could not tolerate the incompetence of my supervisor, and I was not in power to recommend or make changes. I am pleased, for the children's sake, she was removed from this position.

When I resigned my case manager position, I decided to travel to Europe. I visited Ceda and Tika, my mother's neighbors and childhood friends, gentlemen who were like uncles to me when I was without parents. They were eighty-four years old. Even though fifty-five years had passed since the last time they saw me, our meeting resembled my meeting with my brother and sisters. They saw me as the vulnerable child I was when I left Serbia. Their stories of my mother, grandmother, and me as they remembered were wonderful and timely. Seeing them and hearing their memories further filled the voids I felt in my youth. When I got on the airplane to return home, I felt whole.

While traveling home from Switzerland, I had time to think about what I was going to do going forward. It was glorious. Now, when I looked back on my life, I found it was as neat as a menu in a restaurant. I had come far from who I was before I attended college and learned how to organize my life's experiences. At this juncture, I was in a reasonable financial position, but I knew I did not want to retire. While assessing my life as it was at present, I found that my children and grandchildren became my only source of joy. I was cancelling what I wanted to do every time one of them called to ask me to do something for or with them. I loved it when they called me; however, it became apparent to me I was falling back on my past habit of putting others' needs before mine with no boundaries. I realized, by not creating boundaries, I did not form or maintain friendships with peers, so when the children did not need my attention, I was experiencing loneliness. This observation caused me great concern. When I was in turmoil, I was never lonely because turmoil filled my emotional space. I was at peace now, so when I wasn't with the children or grandchildren, the space was empty, and loneliness crept in. Once I acknowledged my realization, I knew I would have to make changes when I returned home. By the time I arrived home, I created a move-forward plan. *Of course!*

My plan was to find a challenging job about one to two hours' drive from my home and family, near enough that I could remain close with the children and grandchildren. I wanted to be independent and break with the familiar places that connected me to the past painful events and people like Ed and Joe. I wanted to make new friends and learn new ways of living and aging. I wanted to see if I was the person I thought I was.

The second day I started my job search, I found a job posting that was written as though someone had read my plan. I had a successful meeting with the board members and promptly started the position within two days of my interview. I embarked on a three-year journey from 2013 to 2016, working as the operations manager for a lovely condominium community on the Siesta Key Beach. A clean slate, perfect for self-examination. I knew no one there. The job came with an ocean-view furnished apartment, so I did not have to disrupt my home in Tampa.

The job was challenging, and I knew, with challenges came great opportunities for success. I resigned when I accomplished my goals. I made a few wonderful friends, and I learned new ideas on how to live and age. I successfully accomplished the responsibilities I was hired to performed. I validated that I was the person I thought I was. This was five months ago. Two months after my resignation, many friends who knew of my experiences encouraged me steadfastly to write my story, thinking it will be interesting to some, helpful to others. I hope they are right.

I traveled for a month and started writing my story. This year, I am sixty-nine years old, enjoying Erikson's stage 8. When I am finished with this book, I will prepare another plan for a new adventure!

I feel whole—three thirds!

CHAPTER TWELVE

I'VE BECOME A YESTERDAY'S WOMAN

I Am a Woman of Substance

It's strange how before I converted my life from chaos to order, I couldn't revisit events in the time frame they occurred because, as discussed in previous chapters, all the events, good and bad, were mixed up like a bad cake recipe. Now, recalling is easier and more pleasant. I have a friend, Connie, who, when she cannot remember something, stops and says something like, "I have it in my brain. I just must find the file." I say I have it in my brain, and I just must find the stage. We both have wisdom, just a different way of expressing it.

It was when I was in Erikson's stage 7, generativity versus stagnation, that I realized I became a yesterday's woman. By age and by experience, I was no longer a young woman. My mother had passed, so I was no longer anyone's child. When she died, I became the matriarch of my family. I was a mother and a grandmother. By my becoming a matriarch, my chief concern naturally became to assist the younger generation in developing and leading useful lives. I reached high levels of responsibility in my professional life, which created opportunities for me to mentor young professionals. Although my life was not perfect, I lived a full life responsibly. I gained a great deal of wisdom from my experiences and from my yesterday's women. I was comfortable with what I learned about myself while in this stage. As I examined my life through the prism of this stage, I realized I became a yesterday's woman and that I belonged to the generativity generation. With me as a yesterday's woman, my responsibility for the remainder of my life is to share my wisdom with the younger generation for them to enrich their lives. I take that responsibility very seriously with great joy.

I Invite You to Grow and Learn from My Experience

To the younger generation, I would like to leave you with the following wisdom. Life is confusing and challenging, because just when you get the answer, life changes the question. Differently stated, our life is constantly moving to different stages. For example, when you are a one-year-old, you are an infant, and when you are three years old, you are a child. When you are twelve years old, you are an adolescent. And so on. For sure, life is not about seeking perfection. If you are not challenged, you are stagnant. Welcome your challenges because they are opportunities to learn and grow. Growth brings great personal power.

Thank You, Dear Friends

Friendship is the greatest treasure a person can have. Happiness is more enjoyable, and burdens are lighter when shared with friends. To my friends, I say, you are my treasure.

Thank You, Teacher

If you are a teacher, I thank you for accepting such a huge responsibility. I remind you that you have the opportunity and the power to help a child who is lost to be found. You can make a profound difference in how a child sees himself or herself. Even when things are overwhelming, show kindness to a lost child; it will be your greatest reward. It has been almost sixty years since I first met Ms. Friedman and Mrs. Whitehorn. In many ways, their kindness and encouragement still affect me in positive ways.

Be a Partner, Not a Cheater

If you are a person, young or old, I remind you to remember, when you engage another person emotionally, you have the responsibility and the obligation to act within the constraints of moral and ethical boundaries. If you can't love a person, leave them. Don't use and deceive them. Life is short. Everyone has the right to live a life full of love and trust. Cheaters breed despair and distrust. Be responsible. Love someone unconditionally.

If You Are Living with a Liar and Cheater

If you are struggling and suffering with a cheater, you have nowhere to go but down. Leave the demoralizing and lonely existence and reclaim your life. Remember to be truthful when telling your story so that you can get the best wisdom from those you are consulting. Remember also, there is always a friend or stranger who will love and stand by you.

Twenty-five years ago, I purchased a life-size leopard statute and placed it in my living room, where I can see it every day, to remind myself that just like the leopards do not change their spots, liars do not stop lying.

If Chaos Prevails in Your Mind,
Seek Ways to Bring Order

In my case, I found Erikson's stages to help me put my mind and life in order. There are many ways of accomplishing this objective, and sometimes it can be as simple as entrusting your story to a friend or a stranger who has experienced life's trials and tribulation. It doesn't matter how you go about it; just go about seeking order. If you seek it, you will find it.

If You Are a Yesterday's Woman
Living an Independent Life

Yesterday's women, whether married or single, were raised to believe the goal in life was to marry, have children, and grow old with their mates to together guide their children as they raise the next generation. Some of you are growing old with your mates and enjoying the fruits of your labor, watching your children and grandchildren as they frolic in your backyard. I compliment you on your hard work and blessings. The rest of us who married wrong and compounded our error by sacrificing our youth while waiting for the wrong marriage to become right, I say, enjoy your independence and believe it is good riddance to the devil who fooled you by disguising himself in men's clothing.

I wish you peace and kindness, dear reader, for I have found, with peace and kindness, you can achieve anything your heart desires.

ABOUT THE AUTHOR

Ms. Djurdjev has a bachelor's degree in psychology, majored in human development and management studies. She places great importance in contributing to the community, and to that end, she was a dedicated court-appointed guardian ad litem and case manager for abused and neglected children. During her tenure, she was recognized by the guardian ad litem program for her dedication to the children and their caretakers who  were involved in the program. She continues to give support to abused and neglected women.

Ms. Djurdjev has over thirty years of successful employee leadership and business management that she gained while managing her consulting business and working for large corporations like Royal Caribbean Cruises and American Airlines and their travel agency partners. She is a licensed realtor and community association manager.

CPSIA information can be obtained
at www.ICGtesting.com
Printed in the USA
FSHW04n0137080318
45216FS